The YOGA SUTRAS *of* PATANJALI

An Accessible Commentary

KURT MATTHYS

The Yoga Sūtras of Patañjali An Accessible Commentary

Kurt Matthys
Cover Design by Hannah Bailey

ISBN-13: 979-8-218-05601-8

About the Author

Kurt Matthys has been practicing, studying, teaching, and lecturing on yoga for 30 years. His primary interest is Indic philosophy, with an emphasis on studying Patañjali's Yoga Sūtras, the Bhagavad Gītā and the Saṃskṛtaṃ (Sanskrit) language. Kurt enjoys lecturing on Patañjali's Yoga Sūtras and teaching proper āsana adjustments to yoga teacher trainees. He has an ERYT 500 registration with Yoga Alliance and has been teaching āsana, prāṇāyāma and meditation classes for over 20 years. Kurt studied with his first teacher Indubala Bhardwaj for 18 years, followed by other teachers. He has traveled to India to spend time in the ancient temples, and has studied at Pattabhi Jois' yoga shala. In addition to being a scholar and practitioner of yoga, and yoga philosophy, Kurt is a practicing Hindu. Join him in discussion in his Facebook group, "Yoga Sutra", a place for philosophy with references to the original, and ancient texts.

Dedications

To Indubala Bhardwaj, without whom I wouldn't be where I am today,
Edwin Bryant, who exposed me to alternatives,
and my wife, Tawn, who put up with me while I wrote this book.

And to all the students over the years that asked me to write this book.

A special thanks for Sabitha Rama for all of her amazing help

And to my reviewers:
Jonathan Kanzelmeyer
Laura Peterson
Nikki Owens
Orah Kittrell
Rachel Kramer
Valerie Diehl

Forward

I have fond memories of my first yoga class led by Kurt. After nearly twenty years, the experience remains etched in my mind...

He was wearing a pair of his signature shiny, bright fluorescent pink yoga pants and a black leotard. He immediately reminded me of Mr. Slim Goodbody from the world of public broadcasting PBS. Using Sanskrit, he counted super slowly on each pose, especially nāvāsana, and it felt like we were in padmāsana for an eternity! I remember thinking "I will never come to this man's class again."

However, I did return to Kurt's class and gratefully, I never stopped going. I enjoyed his humor and yes, his amazing Aṣṭāṅga yoga adventure! I found my confidence as a yoga practitioner growing through the personal interaction and practical guidance Kurt gave me. This cultivated in me a deeper appreciation of the practice and the philosophy behind it. As often as possible, I would spend Friday evenings, and sometimes Saturday afternoons sitting with Kurt in a restaurant booth or in a circle of yogī friends in the studio, listening to him lecture on the Yoga Sutras. The conversations were lively and philosophical, yet spirited and also practical, as we discussed each sūtra's meaning, explored proper Sanskrit pronunciation, and considered how best to apply the sūtras' intentions in our daily lives.

The Yoga Sūtras of Patañjali - An Accessible Commentary is the embodiment of Kurt's own thirty-plus years of self-study or svādhyāya. Svādhyāya, is a Sanskrit word used to describe the practice of self-study and observation (sūtra II.44). As I reflect on the concept of svādhyāya, its meaning, and application, The Yoga Sūtras of Patañjali - An Accessible Commentary is a complementary representation of this concept. "Sva" can mean "self" or "belonging to me," and "adhyāya" can sometimes mean "inquiry", "examination", or "education". In this book, Kurt provides readers with a textual tool, and supplementary resources, that can help them gain a deeper, personal understanding and connection to the philosophy of yoga. Perhaps more importantly, the reading, introspection, and application of the sūtras in Kurt's commentary may encourage readers to live their lives with authenticity and practice yoga with a purpose that extends beyond the goal of attaining a pose (āsana), and instead embraces the attainment of self-discovery and meaning for their life journeys.

Kurt has created a translation for understanding the sūtras in a manner that invites readers to explore each śloka without intimidation. Avoiding abstruse language, Kurt demystifies the Yoga Sūtras while maintaining reverence for its power as an inspirational text, philosophical life guide, and living scripture.

In The Yoga Sūtras of Patañjali - An Accessible Commentary, Kurt masterfully deconstructs each sūtra, its meaning, and transliteration. He provides the readers with a variety of learning resources to help them to understand the context and content of the texts, including an extensive Sanskrit glossary and a Sanskrit pronunciation key.

As a culmination of his own self-studies, and the knowledge he has gained through endless discussions with his teachers and yoga philosophy conversations with friends, Kurt has created a twenty-first-century, modern approach to studying the sūtras. He is not afraid of sharing his personal uncertainties and questions about Patañjali's intentions in the sūtras, which makes his textual commentary even more authentic, and endearing. His questions may even encourage the readers to become more reflective and introspective in their studies.

Kurt possesses the rare quality of teaching challenging āsanas and sequences, and lecturing on yoga philosophy, in a fun, non-judgmental way. His encouraging guidance conveys his passion and love for yoga. Much like his yoga āsana (yogāsana) practice and guidance, Kurt's devotional study of The Yoga Sūtras of Patañjali is deeply profound and commendable. As a Hindu practitioner, and student of Sanskrit, Kurt's dedicated daily reading and meditation on the Yoga Sūtras are inspirational. His commitment to his sūtra studies has influenced his teaching and inspired him to write this book.

Philosophy, let alone yoga philosophy can be quite challenging and cumbersome for many to grasp. However, Kurt's "The Yoga Sūtras of Patañjali" translation is both pragmatic and accessible to all levels of yoga learners and practitioners who wish to study yoga philosophy through an exoteric rather than esoteric lens. Kurt has created an essential and accessible guidebook to help readers understand the yoga sūtras. This book is a phenomenal resource for the yoga community that can be beneficial to yoga teachers, yoga teacher training programs, and yoga practitioners.

Nikki Owens, Ph.D., Owner of Mint Yoga Studio

December 2022

Preface

I've been studying Patañjali's Yoga Sūtras for almost 30 years and lecturing on them for more than half of that time. I own at least fifteen different commentaries on them, both from ancient and contemporary commentators. Patañjali's Yoga Sūtras have dramatically changed my life for the better, and I would like to share what I've learned over the years.

There were three things that caused me to write this book. The first is that there are very few, if any, accessible commentaries on Patañjali that accurately follow what he wrote. There are many 'easy' versions, but they aren't accurate (more on this below). At the opposite end of the spectrum, there are really excellent, philosophical texts, but they tend to be too difficult for people new to Patañjali's Yoga Sūtras, or just new to philosophy. What is needed is a version that is accessible to new students of Patañjali, a version that is a complete text, but written at a level that can be understood. After reading this version, if the student desires to dig deeper into the philosophy, this book will provide a base for such further study. I give a list of a some excellent philosophical books in the introduction.

The second reason that I wrote this is that there are so many inaccurate commentaries on the text. One of the major reasons for inaccuracy is people from other philosophies that want to appropriate Patañjali's teachings, usually modifying what he actually said, so that it fits into their philosophy, thus allowing them to, 1) claim that the text is part of their philosophy, or 2) use it to support their philosophy even when it doesn't. There are commentators that say Patañjali's text is part of their philosophy even when the fundamental metaphysics don't match, and their philosophy is very different from his. I have seen commentators change what Patañjali said in their translation so that it supports their own ideas, or insert their philosophy into the text and claim that theirs is therefore correct.

Others inject content that wasn't in the original text, or distort the meaning, or misrepresent the contextual meaning of the Saṃskṛtaṃ (Sanskrit) by choosing a word from several possible definitions that more closely fits their worldview instead of selecting what more closely represents how Patañjali intended that word to mean.

One of my goals with this book to help disseminate accurate information on what the text is, and is not.

The third reason was the many friends and yoga teacher trainees that I've lectured to over the years that said that I should write and publish my own commentary on Patañjali's sūtras. I started a Facebook group to discuss various Indic philosophies using references to the ancient texts. It was a place for me to post my thoughts, and I just started writing my own commentary and posting it. After I finished posting my comments on the first half of the book, I decided to actually write the book my students had been asking for.

This book is for yoga teachers, yoga teacher trainees, and other people new to Patañjali's Yoga Sutras. In addition to the usual commentary, I've also included, in various places, my own thoughts and personal anecdotes from my own experiences, and other examples to help you understand what Patañjali said, and how it works.

I hope that you will find this book useful. Everything that is correct in the book is due to my various teachers, the excellent commentaries that I've read, and my own thoughts over the years I've been studying the text. All errors are strictly my own.

Table of Contents

Introduction..2
Samādhi Pāda...13
   1.1 Statement of the Topic of the Text..............................13
   I.2 – I.16 Definition of Yoga, Mokṣa, Vṛtti.....................15
   I.17 – I.32 Getting into Samādhi, and Īśvara................27
   I.33 – I.40 Purifying the Mind......................................37
   I.17, I.18, and I.41 – I.51 Samādhi..............................43
Sādhana Pāda...55
   II.1 – II.11 Kriyā Yoga and Kleśas...............................55
   II.12 – II.14 Karma..63
   II.15 – II.28 Cause and Goal of Yoga Sādhana...........67
   II.29 – II.45 The Eight Limbs, Yamas, Niyamas.........81
   II.46 – II.55 Āsana, Prāṇāyāma, Pratyāhāra..............97
Vibhūti Pāda...105
   III.1 – III.12 Dhāraṇā, Dhyāna, Samādhi,...............105
   Pariṇāmas...105
   III.13 – III.15 Characteristics of Prakṛti...................115
   III.16 – III.48 Super-normal Powers.........................119
   III.49 – III.55 More on Attaining Mokṣa...................137
Kaivalya Pāda...143
   IV.1 – IV.6 Miscellaneous...143
   IV.7 – IV.11 Saṃskāras, Vāsanās, Karma, and Rebirth....149
   IV.12 – IV.22 Metaphysics...153
   IV.23 – IV.34 Final thoughts on the Buddhi and Mokṣa....161
Appendix A Devanāgarī Pronunciation.................................170
Appendix B Pronunciation of the Transliteration Marks.........173
Appendix C Thoughts on Jīvanmukti.....................................175
Appendix D Dualism, Non-dualism and Views on Mokṣa.......177
Appendix E Issues with I.42 – I.51..180
Appendix F Sāṃkhya Metaphysics..182
Appendix G Samāpatti vs Samādhi.......................................183
Appendix H Prana...187
Bibliography...189
Glossary...191
Word Index...198

Introduction

Today there are all kinds of things that are called yoga, and unfortunately many of them have nothing to do with yoga. Most people think of yoga as one of two things, either contorting your body into weird positions, or meditating. While yoga does contain both of these things, it's actually a spiritual practice, not an exercise modality. It's a many lifetime practice (yoga assumes reincarnation) and requires dedication and perseverance. It is a personal practice in that it's only about you, the practitioner, and nobody but you can do it for you. The practice requires introspection, personal reflection, and being open to change personal habits and attachments to proceed on the path (sādhana) towards liberation (see the Goal of Yoga later in this introduction).

Some people think that yoga is about social action, saving the planet, helping the poor, etc., but while these are good things, these things don't intrinsically have anything to do with yoga; in fact, from a purist yoga perspective, these things can be considered a distraction. This doesn't mean that a yogī shouldn't do these things, it's that they aren't required to be a yogī.

While there are a number of other philosophies in India that have yoga in the title, when people talk about yoga they mean the Patañjali Yoga Sūtras. There are numerous books in print on the Patañjali yoga sūtras, which most everybody agrees is 'the' discourse on yoga. Existing books tend to be either too philosophical for a first time student of yoga, or way too simplified to be really useful, or they are twisted and warped by people of other philosophies trying to appropriate Patañjali into their own philosophy. What I am attempting to do is to comment on Patañjali's text in an accurate and accessible way for new students to yoga philosophy without watering it down or making it too difficult to understand for first-time readers.

<u>This text will concern itself with Patañjali's metaphysics, practices, and definition of yoga and mokṣa. I will only discuss other philosophies in order to explain Patañjali. Unless otherwise specified, all statements are according to Patañjali. Other philosophies may, or may not disagree with Patañjali.</u>

Very Brief History

Yoga has been in existence for thousands of years. It's mentioned in some of the oldest texts of India. It was practiced by people all over India, by people of all walks of life. Many of the early yogīs were living in caves or in the jungle to get away from the distractions of life in society. In the Rāmāyaṇa, an ancient scriptural text, some advanced yogīs were advisors to kings. They are highly regarded in India. The early yogīs determined, through yogic practices, that everything in life is painful, or unsatisfying if you prefer, and they spent their time in meditation attempting to understand the fundamental nature of the universe and themselves in order to try to figure out how to get rid of the pain. They looked inside themselves, rather than outside, to do this. They figured out that we are not our bodies or our minds, but something eternal, the puruṣa, which is connected to a body made of matter, and that the pain is only in the body and the way to permanently get rid of the pain is to not have a body, i.e. not get reborn again. Yoga is all about the beliefs and associated practices required to get this to happen.

Patañjali and Vyāsa

Patañjali, the author of the yoga sūtras, lived about 2000 years ago and was apparently a highly advanced yogī. This philosophy was not invented by him, but was a systematization of the thinking on yoga at the time. His text on yoga consists of 196 sūtras, depending on which commentary you look at, organized in four chapters/pādas.

He also wrote a text on Ayurveda (Indian medicine) and a commentary on Pānini's grammar of Saṃskṛtam (aka Sanskrit).

Due to the nature of Indic culture, giving dates to historical events is very difficult. Scholars end up attempting to date texts by looking at how they are written and what other texts they reference. For every set of dates someone gives there is at least one other different opinion on those dates. I've seen dates for when Patañjali lived from around 350 BCE to 200 CE. I am not going to justify these dates but just assume that he likely lived somewhere in that time frame.

Vyāsa is the most important commentator on Patañjali, and he lived around 400 CE. This date is also debatable, but I'm not going to argue about that either. The important thing to remember is that his commentary on Patañjali is usually considered canonical, i.e. for the most part nobody argues with him. Many commentators actually comment on Vyāsa's commentary on Patañjali, giving their interpretation of what Vyāsa said. There are also some people that posit that Vyāsa was actually Patañjali, explaining his own text, but nobody knows for sure. I assume that Vyāsa was NOT Patañjali, mostly because that seems to be the prevailing opinion.

Why study Yoga Philosophy?

Why should we study yoga philosophy? Yoga is a collection of practices and beliefs, including ethical and moral ideas, physical postures, breath work, meditation, etc. If we don't know the underpinnings of these practices and beliefs then we don't know if we are actually 'doing' yoga or just what we've been told is 'yoga'. If we do understand the basis of yoga, then we can intelligently decide whether to follow the yogic path or not, and if we do decide to follow it, we will know the 'why' behind everything we do, and can structure our practice accordingly. Then we can justify our actions to ourselves, and to others if we want.

Unfortunately, many people aren't willing to investigate what they believe. Blindly following a philosophy, or belief system, without understanding is a recipe for rigid dogma, and is unfortunately all too common among followers of many philosophies and religions. If someone asks why do you do something, and you don't understand the basis for the action, or even non-action, then the only answer you can give is "just because", or "because I was told that". I once had a discussion with a person that was claiming that certain things were not in the scriptural text for his religion. When I asked him if he had read the text he said no. I told him to read the text and then we could talk about it. He came back a few times saying that a friend of his said that it wasn't in the text, and another time he said that some person lecturing on it said that it wasn't there. I kept asking him if he had read the text and he always said no. I finally said to not come back until he had actually read the book. He never did.

Understanding the basis for your belief system, yoga in particular here, allows you to intelligently think about, discuss, and debate, if you are so inclined, those beliefs. You will understand what the basic assumptions of the belief system are, and think about them, and decide if they make sense to you. After thinking, you can decide to either accept all of the assumptions, just some of them, or none of them (at which time you need to find another belief system). You will also know what is NOT part of the belief system, which is currently important, at least in the yoga world, where there are all kinds of people trying to redefine what yoga is. I was talking to a person that owned a yoga studio and when I mentioned what the goal of yoga was (see below) they said that they didn't want anyone to impose goals on them. This begs the question of why were they running a yoga studio if they didn't even understand or support the goal of yoga?

The Goal of Yoga

The goal of yoga is liberation from suffering, a post-life state that is called mokṣa (II.25). According to the concept of reincarnation, you keep getting reborn until you attain mokṣa. One way to look at this is that you want to not get reborn again. Many of the various Indic philosophies (see below) are considered mokṣa philosophies because they describe a state after death that is permanent and better than being alive.

Mokṣa is a word that is a general concept used for this post-life state; each philosophy has its metaphysics, a set of practices, and its own description/definition of mokṣa. For some, mokṣa is merging with the divine, where others have the idea of just existing without consciousness, and others posit mokṣa as an eternal loving relationship with the divine as a separate entity. **Patañjali's definition of mokṣa is kaivalyam, or absolute aloneness, a blissful state separate and not depending on anything else, forever.**

The goal of yoga is different from the state of yoga and the two should not be confused. The state of yoga is meditation and is explained in sūtra I.2 and the goal of yoga in I.3.

Saṃskṛtam

Patañjali's yoga sūtras were written in the language Saṃskṛtam. While most everybody uses the word Sanskrit, the correct name is Saṃskṛtam, which means 'well formed'. The first 'a' is not pronounced as in 'hat' but as in 'ago'. Sanskrit is a way to identify it and everyone will understand what you mean; it appears to be a western modification of the word. I will use Saṃskṛtam. Please note that they are pronounced the same except that Saṃskṛtam has an 'am' at the end. You pronounce it like Sanskritam.

There are many Saṃskṛtam words that I've left untranslated because they don't translate well, and/or they are very important to the text. I did this because it's important to pronounce the words correctly, especially if you want to sound like you know what you are talking about. I've seen and heard many people pronounce the words incorrectly, mostly I expect, due to hearing them incorrectly, or reading them without the proper transliteration marks. For example, there are three 's's in Saṃskṛtam, 'sh' (ś), 'sh' (ṣ), and 's'. The difference between the two 'sh's is where the sound is coming from. One is in the back of the mouth, at the soft palate and the other at the top of the mouth at the hard palate. At the end of many āsana classes you do śāvāsana (corpse pose). Without the diacritical transliteration marks it looks like 'savāsana', and I've heard many people pronounce it without the 'sh' at the beginning and without the long 'a's (ā), and without the long 'a's in the right place it is also incorrect.

Another example is the word cakra. The 'c' is always pronounced 'ch' in Saṃskṛtam so you would pronounce it as 'chakra'. Many people pronounce this as 'shakra', which means mighty or strong and is used in relation to the god Indra. It has nothing to do with a discus or wheel, which is what cakra means.

The 'a' is never pronounced as in 'hat'. There is no such sound in Saṃskṛtam. I've included a pronunciation guide to Saṃskṛtam in Appendix A and to the transliteration in Appendix B.

The Six Darśanas

There are many different philosophies in India. The most common Hindu philosophies are, rather arbitrarily, divided into six "darśanas", which means vision or view. The six are Vaisheshika (based on atomic theory), Nyāya (based on logic), Sāṃkhya (a very early darśana that Patañjali is based on), Patañjali (also known as Raja Yoga), Purva Mimamsa (a text emphasizing the Vedas, the very earliest texts of Hinduism), and Uttara Mimamsa (also known as Vedānta, of which there are seven different types, a very popular one being Advaita Vedānta). There are also other philosophies, some of which are based on other religions, e.g. Jainism, Sikhism, and Tantra. Buddhism, while not a religion, because the Buddha explicitly denied the existence of God, also has its own philosophy.

Other philosophies use terms differently than Patañjali, and also have different concepts than Patañjali. <u>Everything in this book is according to Patañjali unless it's specifically noted otherwise.</u> Other philosophies are discussed only as necessary to explain Patañjali. All of the above philosophies are attempting to explain the cause of the universe, what our place is in the universe, and what our goal should be in the universe. Patañjali's text is based on Sāṃkhya, which is a very early philosophy which focuses on metaphysics. Patañjali assumes that the reader is aware of Sāṃkhya and builds upon that philosophy, focusing on how to attain mokṣa, or liberation, which is the goal of yoga (more on this below). All of the philosophies that I mentioned above are considered mokṣa philosophies, in that they all describe different visions of the universal metaphysics, and different visions of mokṣa. The only one that is not a mokṣa philosophy is Purva Mimamsa, and is not discussed in this text.

Patañjali's Metaphysics

There are two concepts which are critical to understanding Patañjali. The first is what are the fundamental 'things' that always exist (the ontological entities), and how they cause us to become embodied (<u>see Appendix F</u>). The two types of things are **puruṣa** (an infinite number of them) and **prakṛti**. Everything is created when the two come together. **Puruṣa** is your true/real self, as opposed to your body/mind complex. **Puruṣa** is eternal, unchangeable, and a non-doer: a silent witness. It is pure consciousness. A synonym for **puruṣa** is atman; the two terms are interchangeable. From a Western perspective, especially Christian, the **puruṣa** is akin to your soul, which is not entirely accurate, but close enough for this text.

Prakṛti is everything other than the **puruṣa**. It's matter: all the 'stuff' of the universe. It includes **gross matter** that you can touch, and **subtle matter**, which you can't touch or see, but does exist. **Prakṛti** includes your intellect, ego, the powers of the senses of action (speaking, grasping, moving, excreting, procreating) and knowledge (hearing, touching, tasting, seeing, smelling), and the part of your mind that interfaces with the senses. The organs of the senses, both action and knowledge, are gross matter (see pages 53 and 54 in Swāmī Niranjanānanda's book). All this is explained in great detail in the Sāṃkhya Kārikā if you are interested.

Patañjali accepts the Sāṃkhya metaphysics and builds on the Sāṃkhya philosophy. Sāṃkhya details how all the things in the universe get created as devolutes of **prakṛti** (see Appendix F). The basic idea is that when **puruṣa** touches/contacts **prakṛti**, you get creation. The first devolute is **buddhi**, the intellect. The **buddhi** is a discriminator, deciding the value of sensory input and determining what to do with it. From the **buddhi** comes the ego (**ahaṃkāra**). This is a sense of self and has nothing to do with the Freudian concept of ego. It's simply the idea of an I and a not I. From the **ahaṃkāra** comes the powers of the senses of action and knowledge, **manas** (the part of the mind that handles sensory input and passes it to the **buddhi** to decide what to do with it), **subtle matter**, and **gross matter**. **Gross matter** is what we can perceive with our physical senses. **Subtle matter** is the cause of **gross matter**, while it exists, it's not perceivable by our physical senses. Please note that neither Sāṃkhya nor Patañjali explain what caused **puruṣa** to touch/contact **prakṛti**; they just assume that the contact is beginingless.

Most commentators use the word evolute instead of devolute. Bhārati, in his second edition of his commentary on the first chapter of Patañjali, prefers devolute, and I tend to agree with that. The reason for using devolute is that we are trying to escape **gross matter** and evolve 'up' the 'devolution tree' mentioned above, from **gross matter** to **puruṣa** to get the knowledge necessary to attain mokṣa. So moving 'down' the tree, away from **puruṣa**, is a devolution, not an evolution. But this is a semantic matter and you can use either one as you wish.

Reincarnation

Reincarnation is one of the fundamental assumptions of Indic philosophy, and means that you keep getting reborn until you attain mokṣa (except for Purva Mimamsa which also assumes reincarnation but is not interested in mokṣa). Sāṃkhya and Patañjali both assert that life is suffering and pain, and that the reason for a person to take up the yogic path to attain mokṣa is to relieve this suffering and pain, which only exists when you are alive; if you are not born again you won't have any suffering. The idea of mokṣa is to know how to not get born again. Instead of the words 'suffering or pain', another word that can be used is 'unsatisfying', which emphasizes that while there is pleasure in the world, it's impermanent and not fully satisfying, and thus painful. It also says that pain is both mental and physical.

Citta

Citta is a Saṃskṛtam word used by Patañjali that means the mind. It has three parts, the intellect (buddhi), the ego (ahaṃkāra), and the part of the mind that interfaces with the sensory input (manas). As noted in the Metaphysics section earlier, the manas takes sensory input, identifies it, and passes it up to the buddhi. The buddhi then decides what to do with the input, to act or not to act. The ahaṃkāra is the idea of a 'me' as different from 'you', and is completely different from the Freudian idea of the ego.

An important distinction between puruṣa and citta is that, while the citta is intelligent, it's not conscious. It only seems to be conscious because of its association/conjunction with puruṣa.

Sūtra

Another important word to understand is sūtra, which means thread. Patañjali's text consists of about 196 sūtras, strung together as threads, and are not necessarily complete sentences. I said 'about 196' because in some commentaries there are one or two sūtras missing. The sūtra style of writing is extremely terse, so as to make it much easier to memorize. Authors of sūtra texts work hard to get rid of every possible syllable and still get their point across. The side effect of this style is that it's so terse that it's almost impossible to understand without commentary. You can think of the sūtras as the bullet points in a slide presentation.

Note that in the sūtra style of writing, things in a list are in order of importance with the first being the most important and the last being the least important.

Yoga and gender

Historically yoga was practiced almost exclusively by men, even though there were some very famous female yogīs. The Saṃskṛtaṃ language has the concept of male, female, and neuter words. So you have yogī (male) and yoginī (female), although yogī can also be used for women. Since according to yoga and reincarnation we are a puruṣa, without sex or gender, that currently has a body (until we attain mokṣa), and the sex/gender can and does change from life to life, I will just use the word yogī to refer all people following the yogic path (sādhana). Sādhana is the set of beliefs and practices that you use to attain mokṣa. This book is all about that path.

Structure of Patañjali's Text

Patañjali's main idea is to purify your mind, so that you can meditate. Samādhi is a 'tool' used during meditation to get the knowledge you need to attain mokṣa. To support this, Patañjali's text is organized into four pādas (chapters). The first chapter is about the definition of yoga, the definition of mokṣa, and all about samādhi. The second chapter is a 'cookbook' on how to get to samādhi, and discusses obstacles, karma, and the first five of his well known eight limbs of Aṣṭāṅga Yoga. The eight limbs are:

1. yama – ethical restraints
2. niyama – observances and attitudes
3. āsana – postures
4. prāṇāyāma – increasing/expanding prāṇa in the body
5. pratyāhāra – withdrawing from the senses
6. dhāraṇā – concentration
7. dhyāna – meditation
8. samādhi – tool for getting discriminative wisdom (viveka khyātiḥ) while in meditation

The third chapter defines the various 'levels' of meditation, which are the last three limbs of Aṣṭāṅga Yoga, the super-normal powers you can obtain through consistent practice, and finishes up with more on mokṣa. The fourth chapter is a collection of clarifications and additional information that was not in the first three chapters.

Further reading

If, after reading this text, you want to delve into the philosophy more deeply, I would suggest starting with Edwin Bryant's truly excellent book "The Yoga Sūtras of Patañjali". I would also suggest Swāmī Hariharānanda Āraṇya's book "Yoga Philosophy of Patañjali". Pandit Usharbudh Arya wrote an excellent and extremely detailed book on the first pāda/chapter of Patañjali "Yoga Sūtras of Patañjali Volume I". He changed his name to

Swāmī Veda Bhārati when he wrote a book on the second chapter, "Yoga Sūtras of Patañjali Volume II". Unfortunately, he died before writing on the third and fourth chapters. Another book that I like is "Patañjali's Yoga sūtras" by Rama Prasada; this book is Rama's translation of Vachaspati Mishra's (a well-known commentator) commentary on Patañjali.

Final introductory thoughts

In his philosophy, Patañjali discusses different topics in groups of sūtras, and I've organized my text around these groups of sūtras. One of the problems that I've seen is that commentators tend to explain the sūtras one-at-a-time and don't put them together and explain them as groups. This, in my opinion, makes the text more difficult to understand. Many sūtras build upon each other and, therefore, don't make sense in isolation. They should be discussed together.

In this book I give the Saṃskṛtaṃ devanāgarī script, a transliteration (see Appendix B for pronunciation of each character), and a translation of the words of each sūtra in the order they are in the Saṃskṛtaṃ, and then I comment on them. In the transliteration I remove all the sandhis, which are Saṃskṛtaṃ rules that change/modify letters so that it sounds good, among other things. If you don't know about sandhis don't worry about them. I continually reference other sūtras in my commentary to help you understand how all of it fits together into a whole philosophy. I also have an introduction and summary to each section.

Some of the pages have more white space at the bottom than others. This is because I wanted the devanāgarī, transliteration, translation, and the first lines of the commentary of every sūtra to all be on the same page.

So let's get started.

Samādhi Pāda

1.1 Statement of the Topic of the Text

I.1 अथ योगानुशासनम्

atha yoga anu śāsanam

"now, yoga, following/continuing, teachings"

Most sūtra texts start with a statement of what the text is going to be about. Patañjali says that he's going to talk about yoga. Note that he didn't make it up; he just wrote down what the current yoga thinking was at the time. This is evident in the prefix 'anu' which means 'within/following/ continuing', so he's saying here that he's just continuing existing teaching. He is also systematizing them. In the Kaṭha Upaniṣad, an earlier text (before Patañjali, somewhere between the first and fifth century BCE), in Chapter 6, ślokas 10 and 11, it says:

> 10. When the five senses are stilled, with the manas, and the intellect is not moving, that is called the highest state.
> 11. They think that is yoga, when the senses are carefully held steady; yoga becomes both the source [of mokṣa] and the vanishing [of bondage].

Śloka 10 is a description of what Patañjali calls samādhi: a special, very deep meditation that we'll get more into later. In this śloka, the stilling of the senses, manas (part of the citta), and intellect (buddhi) suggests that no thinking is going on. The use of "that is called the highest state", indicates that Yoga was already known when this Upaniṣad was written, which was before Patañjali.

Śloka 11 talks about samādhi again. In this śloka, the "source [of mokṣa]" is the puruṣa (i.e. your true self) coming to abide in it's own form, and "vanishing [of bondage]" is the removal of the connection between puruṣa and prakṛti (everything other than puruṣa). These will be discussed later in this book.

The point here is that it shows that Patañjali didn't make this up.

Samādhi Pāda

Remember that Patañjali's philosophy is not the only text with 'yoga' in the title. It is, however, the text that everybody means when they discuss yoga philosophy. Also, remember that another name for this philosophy is Raja Yoga, or King/Royal Yoga.

I.2 – I.16 Definition of Yoga, Mokṣa, Vṛtti

In this section Patañjali gives his definition of yoga, mokṣa/liberation, and what you need to do to attain mokṣa. Please note that this pāda/chapter is mainly for highly advanced yogīs. The second chapter is more of a how-to for the rest of us.

I.2 योगश्चित्त वृत्ति निरोधः

> yogaḥ citta vṛtti nirodhaḥ
>
> "yoga is, the mind, fluctuations, restraint/control/stopping"

Patañjali defines yoga as the stopping of the fluctuations of the citta, which is meditation. If your mind isn't moving, you are meditating. Vyāsa, in his commentary on I.1 specifically says that yoga is samādhi. Samādhi is a special, very deep meditation that we'll get into later. So the state of yoga is meditation/ samādhi. Don't confuse samādhi with the goal of yoga, which is mokṣa. <u>Yoga is NOT 'union' as many people think; it's meditation</u> (see my comments below on the meaning of the word yoga). According to Patañjali, you use meditation to attain mokṣa, and he spends the rest of the book discussing this.

As I mentioned in the Introduction, the citta is the mind, and consists of the buddhi (the intellect), the ahaṃkāra (the ego: the sense of "I" or "me", and the manas (the part that interfaces with the senses).

Vṛttis are fluctuations of the citta, and for the most part are thoughts. The exception is the vṛtti of sleep (I.10). Patañjali discusses and defines them in I.5 – I.11.

Meaning of the Word Yoga

We need to have an understanding of the meaning of the word yoga. In this sūtra, Patañjali defines yoga as meditation. However, in the past I've had teachers say that yoga means 'union', or 'union of the body and mind' or something else like that. I always had the same question about that definition: what does that get me, and how is it useful? I was never satisfied with that definition. <u>Later, after studying Patañjali, I found that the definition according to Patañjali is very different, and much more satisfying, i.e. meditation. It has nothing to do with union.</u>

There are numerous definitions for the word 'yoga' in the unabridged Apte dictionary, one of which is "joining" and another is "application or concentration of the thoughts, abstract contemplation, meditation, (esp.) self-concentration, abstract meditation, and mental abstraction practiced as a system (as taught by Patañjali and called the Yoga Philosophy)."

This sūtra is "yogaś citta vṛtti nirodhaḥ", which literally means yoga is the stilling of the fluctuations of the chitta/mind. When your mind is stilled, you are meditating; you aren't joining anything. This is also, as I mentioned above, emphasized by Vyāsa's commentary on the first sūtra where he states that yoga is samādhi. This is unequivocal. Please note that this is not the definition of the word in some other philosophies, but it is according to Patañjali, and we're only concerned with Patañjali in this text.

The word yoga comes from the Saṃskṛtam root word 'yuj.' From page 147 and 148 in Swāmī Veda Bhārati's second edition of the first chapter:

"The word [yoga] can be derived from 'yuj' in several forms as follows:

- 'yuj' of the fourth conjugation (yujyate), meaning samādhi
- 'yujir' of the sixth conjugation (yunakti), meaning samādhi
- 'yuj' of the tenth conjugation (yojayati), meaning 'to join", or 'to restrain', or 'to keep under control, as in yoking'

The English word 'yoke' is acknowledged by the Oxford English Dictionary to be cognate to 'yuj', and so is the word 'join'. 'Yoke' is derived from the third 'yuj' in the above list; 'join' is from the second, but its meaning is from the third. Ancient Vedic texts use the former two as meaning 'to experience samādhi '. According to Vyāsa, the word yoga in Patañjali is derived not from the 'yuj' of yoking or joining, but from the verbs meaning samādhi."

Feuerstein says that 'union' is definitely not applicable to Patañjali's yoga. He also says that the essence of the philosophy is 'disunion', or the separation of puruṣa and prakṛti.

I.3 तदा द्रष्टुः स्वरूपेऽवस्थानम्

tadā draṣṭuḥ sva rūpe avasthānam
"then, of the seer, own, form, abiding/remaining"

In I.2 Patañjali said that yoga is stilling your mind. Here he continues by saying that if you still your mind you can attain the state of mokṣa: <u>the goal of yoga, which is to disconnect your puruṣa completely from prakṛti</u>; another way to put this is that you won't be reborn. Disconnecting from prakṛti is what happens when you 'know' the difference between puruṣa and prakṛti, master asamprajñāta samādhi (we'll get to that later) and attain mokṣa/liberation. Remember that this is not just stilling it for a second, nor is it easy. You need to be able to still your mind at will for as long as you want to get this knowledge, and this takes years/lifetimes of practice.

Remember that your puruṣa is simply consciousness, so that when it disconnects from prakṛti the only thing that it's conscious of is itself. Since it's not connected to prakṛti/matter anymore it's abiding in its own form. 'Abide' means to remain/continue/stay and implies, at least in this case, that this state is forever. And once you attain mokṣa, why would you ever want to leave that blissful state?

Patañjali uses several different words for puruṣa, and here he uses 'seer' as in 'the one that sees'. Your puruṣa is considered to be the seer, looking at prakṛti through your mind, while everything in prakṛti is considered the 'seen'.

Many people say that samādhi is easy. This is not true. I've had runners say that they get into samādhi when running and they are 'in the zone'. This is not samādhi; it's the mind running on autopilot, and it does keep fluctuating as it keeps the person running down the right roads, etc. Or I've heard that someone said that they were in samādhi during a car accident because they are totally focused on what's going on. This is not samādhi; it's the mind focusing on one thing, but not intentionally with the goal of attaining mokṣa. I've even heard that samādhi is a 'natural' state of the mind and therefore you don't have to work at it; it just happens when the time is right. While samādhi may be a 'natural' state of the mind, it's not easy – just ask any long-time meditator. Samādhi is an intentional thing where the yogī is purposefully stilling the mind so that it rests on the object of meditation, and only the object of meditation for the purpose of attaining mokṣa.

I.4 वृत्ति सारूप्यं इतरत्र

vṛtti sārūpyam itaratra

"fluctuations, identification with, elsewhere"

In I.3 Patañjali said that when you still your mind properly, you will attain mokṣa/liberation. Here he says that if you don't still your mind, you identify yourself with your body and mind and its interactions with the world, i.e. prakṛti. This is the 'elsewhere' in the sūtra. You identify with your sex, job, size, shape, intelligence, etc., none of which is the real you, i.e. the puruṣa.

I.5 वृत्तयः पञ्चतय्यः क्लिष्टाक्लिष्टाः

vṛttayaḥ pañcatayyaḥ kliṣṭa akliṣṭāḥ

"fluctuations, five-fold, not helpful, helpful"

In I.2 Patañjali said that you need to still your vṛttis. Now he's going to talk about them. In this sūtra he says that there are five types, and they are either helpful or not helpful: akliṣṭa or kliṣṭa. There are a number of different translations of the word kliṣṭa, such as painful, detrimental, harmful, damaging, afflicted. I prefer 'not helpful.' The opposite of kliṣṭa, akliṣṭa, helpful, is noted by the 'a' added at the beginning of the word. This is standard in Saṃskṛtam, and in many cases in English, e.g. theist vs. atheist.

<u>The kliṣṭa vṛttis are not helpful as they pull you away from your sādhana, while the akliṣṭa ones help you stay on the path towards mokṣa.</u> Note that some vṛttis can be helpful at one time and not helpful later. For example, if you are in Cincinnati and want to get to Columbus but don't know how to get there, a map to Columbus is very helpful. However, once you get to Columbus, it's not helpful anymore.

Please note that, while there are only five types, there are an infinite number of vṛttis. Patañjali also does not attach moral judgments/values to them like good and bad. He's just saying that all of them fit into one of these types. Yes, it's possible to come up with some that don't really fit, but what he's trying to do is to define them in general categories so you can understand them.

I.6 प्रमाण विपर्यय विकल्प निद्रा स्मृतयः

pramāṇa viparyaya vikalpa nidrā smṛtayaḥ
"right knowledge, misconception, imagination, sleep, memory"

Here he just lists the 5 types of vṛttis. Then in I.7 – I.11 he discusses each one.

- pramāṇa – right knowledge
- viparyaya – misconception
- vikalpa – imagination
- nidrā – sleep
- smṛti – memory

I.7 प्रत्यक्षानुमानागमाः प्रमाणानि

pratyakṣa anumāna āgamāḥ pramāṇāni
"sense perception, inference, testimony, right knowledge"

The first vṛtti is pramāṇa, or right knowledge. There are three sources of right knowledge that Patañjali accepts. Other philosophies accept different numbers of sources. The three sources of right knowledge are 1) pratyakṣa, direct sensory perception which is seeing, feeling, hearing, etc., 2) anumāna, inference, and 3) āgama, testimony (a reliable person or text).

I.8 विपर्ययो मिथ्या ज्ञानमतद्रूप प्रतिष्ठम्

viparyaya mithyā jñānam a tat rūpa pratiṣṭham
"misperception, false, knowledge, not, that, form, established"

Viparyaya, is misperception, or perceiving something as it is not ("established" here means in your mind). For example, the very traditional snake in the road: If you are walking down a road in India at sundown and see a snake in the road, you'll make a wide path around it because snakes in India tend to be very poisonous. However, when you get to the other side of the snake and look back with the sun behind you, you can see that it's actually a rope. The same thing applies to all five senses.

I.9 शब्द ज्ञानानुपाती वस्तु शून्यो विकल्पः

śabda jñāna anupātī vastu śūnyaḥ vikalpaḥ
"words, knowledge, resulting from, real object, devoid of, imagination"

The first word of this sūtra 'śabda' (words), says that this one is based strictly on words, not seeing or hearing, etc.

Vikalpa has a bunch of different translations, verbal delusion, imagination, logical construction, fancy, conceptualization. So vikalpa is knowledge based on, or resulting from words, where there is no real object (devoid of a real object) behind the words. Because of this I prefer to translate it as imagination. An example of this is if I say that I saw a dragon walking down the street, you know exactly what I mean even though dragons don't exist. Imagination is necessary for developing anything new since you need words to discuss what the new thing is before you build it.

Another example is time. While it 'exists', you can't see or touch time so it fits into this category. Time is a useful concept in that it allows us to order events as before or after, or as past, present, and future. But there is no 'real object' to time.

There's also a different facet to vikalpa in phrases that are commonly used but are meaninless, e.g. time flies, and a cloth made out of turtle hair. Neither of these have real objects; time doesn't have wings, and there's no such thing as turtle hair. But each of these phrases cause a vṛtti in the mind.

I.10 अभाव प्रत्ययालम्बना वृत्तिर्निद्रा

abhāva pratyaya ālambanā vṛttiḥ nidrā
"absence, cause, support, state, sleep"

In Indic philosophy, there are two kinds of sleep: nidrā which is deep sleep, while svapna (not used in this sūtra) is dreaming. Therefore, this sūtra is about deep sleep. In deep sleep, or non-REM sleep, you aren't dreaming and your mind is perfectly still, but this is still considered a vṛtti according to Bhārati.

Some translations say that it's the absence of nothing, or something like that. Vyāsa says that, even though you were sleeping and not aware, when you wake up you can say that you slept well or that you slept poorly. You couldn't do this if your mind was completely inactive. Bharati says that, if you get cold at night, you wake up, cover yourself, and go back to sleep without remembering it until you get up. He gives another example: if you are in deep sleep and someone calls your name, and you wake up. If your mind is completely inactive during deep sleep, what causes you to cover up when you are cold, and what causes you to wake up when someone calls your name? Since, given these examples, there must be some part of your mind that is still active, there must be vṛttis in deep sleep.

Bryant says that dream sleep falls in the category of memory (the next vṛtti), since it involves the activation of saṃskāras.

I.11 अनुभूत विषयासंप्रमोषः स्मृतिः

anubhūta viṣaya asaṃpramoṣaḥ smṛttiḥ
"experienced, objects, not being lost, memory"

This sūtra defines smṛti or memory. We all know what this means, but the translations and the actual sūtra are trying to define it, which results in some strange translations.

So now that we know what all the types of vṛttis are, we need to understand that while there are only five types, there are an infinite number of vṛttis, as opposed to the kleśas discussed in the second chapter, where there are only 5 kleśas.

I.12 अभ्यास वैराग्याभ्यां तन्निरोधः

abhyāsa vairāgyābhyām tat nirodhaḥ
"practice, dispassion/non-attachment from both, their, stilling"

Now that we know what all the five types of vṛttis are, we need to know how to still them as Patañjali mentioned in I.2. <u>Here he says that to still the vṛttis, you need to do two things: practice and have non-attachment.</u> Patañjali spends the next four sūtras explaining these two important concepts. Here "stilling" is referencing the stilling of the vṛttis as mentioned in I.2.

I.13 तत्र स्थितौ यत्नोऽभ्यासः

tatra sthitau yatnaḥ abhyāsaḥ
"of these, in the matter of settling, effort, practice"

In the previous sūtra, Patañjali said that you need practice and dispassion to still the vṛttis. Here he is defining abhyāsa/practice, the effort you put forth in order to still the mind, i.e. get rid of the vṛttis. He's saying that there is effort in the practice; it doesn't just happen.

I.14 स तु दीर्घ काल नैरन्तर्य सत्करासेवितो दृढ भूमिः

saḥ tu dīrgha kāla nairantarya satkara āsevitaḥ dṛḍha bhūmiḥ
"that, but, long, time, without interruption, respect, practiced, firm,
  ground"

In I.14 Patañjali adds to the previous sūtra, saying, that you only reach a firm ground from practice (that) when you have practiced for a long time (months and years) without interruption and with the proper attitude/respect to the practice. So, if it's Wednesday evening, and your favorite TV show is not on, so you decide to practice; this is NOT what he's talking about. This practice takes many lifetimes. As a yoga teacher I ask every new student how long they've been practicing and the answer is almost always "off and on for x years". This also means more 'off' than 'on'. That is also not considered by Patañjali to be abhyāsa/practice.

He also mentions that you need the proper attitude/respect to the practice. What he means is that you have to understand what you're doing and why. If you don't have that, you aren't able to focus your efforts towards achieving the goal, which is mokṣa.

In Encinitas, California a few years ago, the local school board brought yoga into the physical education department. Naturally there was a lawsuit saying that the school was indoctrinating their children into a religion that some parents didn't like, and moreover, it's not possible to take the spirituality out of the practice. The yoga community responded that yes, it's possible to take the spirituality out of the practice. The courts ruled in favor of the yoga community, but in my opinion, both sides lost. The anti-yoga parents lost because yoga was still in the school, but more importantly, the yoga community lost because yoga is fundamentally a spiritual practice and if you remove the spirituality what you have left is exercise that looks like yoga but isn't.

There is a valid idea that just doing āsana, or chanting mantra, or meditating just to calm your mind can also lead you to the yogic path. While you might not start being interested in a spiritual journey, just doing the practices, for whatever reason, can bring you to the yogic path. I heard someone once say, "Yoga doesn't ask you to buy, or buy into, anything. It just says practice, you'll figure it out." Many of the yoga teachers that I've lectured to decided to do teacher training because they want to understand what they're doing, deepening their practice, and aren't interested in teaching at all.

I.15 दृष्टानुश्रविक विषय वितृष्णस्य वशीकार संज्ञा वैराग्यम्

dṛṣṭa anuśravika viṣaya vitṛṣṇasya vaśīkāra saṃjñā vairāgyam
"seen, heard in scriptural texts, sense objects, of one that is free from desire, subduing, consciousness, dispassion/non-attachment"

In this, and the next sūtra he talks about non-attachment. Here he says that it's when you have no desire for things seen and heard, e.g. women/men, food, drink, power, and things in scripture. What he's saying here is that you have no craving (you're not attached) to material things or getting to heaven or anything else in scripture. People that followed the Vedas made sacrifices to get things from the gods, and so they would go to the heavenly realms to enjoy the fruit of their good/dharmic actions, get born again, and do it again, ad infinitum. So you need to be ascetic, wanting little, and only being concerned with your sādhana (your yogic path) so you can attain mokṣa (notice that we are back to the goal of yoga again).

I want to point out that dispassion doesn't mean that yogīs are dull, miserable people. Most people live going from happy to sad and back. Yogīs live in a state of bliss that surpasses the happiness that normal people have. They do enjoy whatever is available but aren't upset when good things aren't available. My favorite example of this is a picture in one of the meditation halls at the Satchidānanda Ashram in Yogaville. It's a picture of Swāmī Satchidānanda riding a horse through a field. His long beard is split into two halves and streaming out behind him on each side of his head, and he has an ear-to-ear grin on his face. While he enjoyed it, he wasn't attached to it.

I.16 तत्परं पुरुष ख्यातेर्गुण वैतृष्ण्यम्

tat param puruṣa khyāteḥ guṇa vaitrishnyam
"that, highest/ultimate, self, wisdom, qualities of matter, indifference"

Here Patañjali finishes discussing dispassion/non-attachment by saying that the ultimate dispassion/non-attachment is when you don't desire anything in prakṛti. This is because you only care about your practice, where the goal is to get completely away from prakṛti. You realize that stuff is just stuff and not you; the newest smart phone won't help you to attain mokṣa.

Patañjali introduces a new word in this sūtra: guṇa. This is an important concept that you should understand, as it comes up later in the text too. All of prakṛti, which is everything other than puruṣa, and includes your mind, gross, and subtle matter, can be described with three qualities:

1) sattva – calm, peaceful, light
2) rajas – heat, energy, activity, movement
3) tamas – inactivity, steadiness, dullness, heaviness

These three things are qualities, not objects that you can touch or look at. Some people think these qualities are things, but they're not. They are ways to describe the qualities of material objects.

In your path (sādhana) to attaining mokṣa you want to get rid of rajas and tamas in your mind so that you can be sattvic, which allows you to meditate better. This isn't to say that rajas and tamas are always negative. For example, you want your house furnace to be rājasic to heat your house, and you want the bricks in the walls to be very tāmasic so they stay put and don't fall down. Patañjali is only interested in purifying your mind, by meditating, so that you can get the knowledge you need to attain mokṣa. When meditating you want your mind to be calm and peaceful, i.e. sattvic. Rajas and tamas just disturb your meditation.

<u>Now, all this is a process and it doesn't happen overnight.</u> I had one student who was in tears when we were discussing non-attachment because she thought that it meant that she couldn't love her new baby. This is not what it's about. If you are born a highly advanced yogī, from work in previous lives, you won't be interested in having a relationship, or sex, or the newest cell phone, or whatever. If you aren't a highly advanced yogī, you will most likely be a householder and be interested in a spouse, kids, and a job. You can work on your sādhana, but it's harder because of these distractions and their associated attachments. This is where most of us are.

The question of how you can be attached to your sādhana when Patañjali says that you need to be unattached frequently comes up. The answer is that you should not be attached to anything in prakṛti; since your sādhana is to separate your prakṛtic body from your puruṣa, there's no problem here.

<u>Section Summary</u>

This section gives the definition of yoga (samādhi), the goal of yoga (mokṣa), and discusses the vṛttis and how to get rid of the kliṣṭa vṛttis: practice (abhyāsa) and non-attachment/dispassion (vairāgyaṃ).

Why do we need to get rid of the vṛttis? Because the kliṣṭa vṛttis keep you focused on the guṇas, i.e. prakṛti/things/stuff, and therefore keep you from attaining mokṣa. And when you have vṛttis you can't be in samādhi, (your mind can't move in samādhi), which is the tool that you need to get the knowledge of your real self (puruṣa), and totally disconnect from prakṛti to attain mokṣa. You do want to keep the akliṣṭa (helpful) vṛttis when you aren't in samādhi because they help you keep moving towards mokṣa. However, you need to get rid of even the akliṣṭa (helpful) ones in the end to actually attain mokṣa. Patañjali discusses this at the end of this chapter.

I.17 – I.32 Getting into Samādhi, and Īśvara

After discussing the state of yoga, the goal of yoga, the vṛttis and how to get rid of them via practice and non-attachment, Patañjali spends the rest of the first chapter on samādhi. First, he defines the two major types of samādhi, samprajñāta (with an object of meditation) and asamprajñāta (without an object of meditation), in I.17 and I.18. He does this as a segue to sūtras I.19 – I.40. **I will give only a quick discussion of these two types of samādhi here and go into more detail of I.17 and I.18 in my discussion of I.41 – I.51.** As I mentioned before, samādhi is a 'tool' that you use to get the wisdom you need to attain mokṣa. It's a very deep, special, meditation, where the idea of 'I am meditating on that' is lost, and only 'that' remains in your mind.

Patañjali defines samprajñāta samādhi to have four levels or stages and asamprajñāta samādhi has only one. The major difference between these two is that with samprajñāta you are meditating on something, and in asampra-jñāta there is no object to meditate on. For this section of the sūtras though, the only important thing is samprajñāta samādhi. Patañjali explains the various levels of samprajñāta samādhi in I.41 – I.50 and asamprajñāta in I.51. He also defines samādhi in III.3.

In I.19 – I.32 Patañjali discusses different ways to get to samādhi, and how the concept of Īśvara (i.e. the divine) fits into the philosophy. I'll discuss this in sūtra I.23.

I.19 भव प्रत्ययो विदेह प्रकृति लयानाम्

bhava pratyayaḥ videha prakṛti layānām
"material existence, cause, bodiless, matter, clinging/sticking/merged
    in"

Here he says that advanced yogīs known as videhās and prakṛti-layas get to samādhi by being reborn or when their saṃskāras 'turn back on' so that they can continue their sādhana. All the commentators I have read agree that these two types of beings are highly advanced yogīs, but after that they seem to disagree as to just what exactly they are. The videhās are bodiless ones and the prakṛti-layas are enmeshed in prakṛti. I have never seen a good description and explanation of these, but that's not really the point here. The point is that they can get into samādhi due to their nature at some point.

I.20 श्रद्धा वीर्य स्मृति समाधि प्रज्ञा पूर्वक इतरेषां

śraddhā vīrya smṛti samādhi prajñā pūrvakaḥ itareṣāṃ

"faith, vigor, memory, samādhi, discernment, for others"

In I.19 Patañjali said that the videhās and prakṛti-layas get to samādhi by their own nature. In I.20 <u>he says that for the rest of us we get to samādhi by faith (in the practice), vigor (virya that you get from celibacy noted in II.30 and II.38), memory, samādhi (needed to get into asamprajñāta), and discernment. The implication here is that we have to work at it.</u> There also seems to be disagreement as to whether Patañjali is talking about getting into samprajñāta or asamprajñāta samādhi. I think he's talking about both of them since we need these things to get into samprajñāta and still need them to get into asamprajñāta, at which time we don't need them anymore.

I.21 तीव्र संवेगानामासन्नः

tīvra saṃvegānām āsannaḥ

"intense, those with intensity, imminent"

This sūtra and the next one give some information about how long it takes to get to samādhi. It's very simple: intense practice by those who work intensely makes samādhi imminent. All Patañjali is saying is that, the harder you work at your sādhana, the sooner you get to samādhi. The point to take from this is that you have to work at it.

Vyāsa breaks yogīs up into three groups of three, where the three main groups are people that work at their sādhana mildly, medium, and intensely. He breaks each of these groups into three sub-types of mild, medium, and intense. His comments here apply to this sūtra and the next one.

I.22 मृदु मध्याधिमात्रत्वात् ततोऽपि विशेषः

mṛdu madhya adhimātratvāt tataḥ api viśeṣaḥ

"mild, medium, extreme, possessed by those, therefore, also, distinction"

Here Patañjali says that even among the yogīs with intensity, that intensity can be broken down into mild, medium, and extreme intensity. What he is saying in this and the previous sūtra is basically that the more effort you put into your sādhana, the faster you are going to progress.

I.23 ईश्वर प्रणिधानाद्वा

Īśvara praṇidhānāt vā

"God, devotion/surrender to, or"

Now we actually get to Īśvara. Patañjali says "Īśvara praṇidhānād va", "or by surrender to Īśvara". Praṇidhāna is actually two words, 'prani' which means 'to offer', and 'dhana' which is 'anything that is of value to you', or 'your dearest treasure'. So you are offering/surrendering your most precious treasure, i.e. yourself, to Īśvara. In fact, in II.45 he says that from surrendering to Īśvara you will get the perfection of samādhi. This is right after II.44 where he says that by study of scripture (svādhyāya) you will get 'closer' or 'establish a connection with' your deity of choice, your iṣṭa devatā.

I translated Īśvara as God here. 'God' is not really accurate so I'm going to leave this word untranslated hereafter. The word Īśvara is made up of two words, 'ish' and 'vara', where 'ish' means 'master of' and 'vara' means 'best/most-beautiful/finest', so the word itself means the master of the best. Īśvara is a term with many nuances in Hinduism which are not important for Patañjali's text. Various commentators have defined the term Īśvara in various ways depending on their own philosophy.

In this sūtra he says that you can surrender to Īśvara as an alternative to getting to samādhi by being a videhā or prakṛti-laya as mentioned in I.19, or by the methods in I.20, i.e. faith, vigor, memory, etc. If you are not theistically inclined you can use the methods in I.20. If you are theistically inclined you can surrender to Īśvara to get to samādhi.

I have heard and read some people say that practicing Īśvara praṇidhāna is easier than other methods, but I don't necessarily agree with that. Surrendering here requires completely getting rid of your ego, which is very difficult, so while I agree that Īśvara praṇidhāna is an alternative, it's not necessarily easier. But this sūtra shows that, in yoga, there are many paths to attain the goal, i.e. mokṣa.

Since he introduced Īśvara here, Patañjali needs to describe Īśvara, which he does in the next four sūtras. The attributes he assigns to Īśvara are all applicable to most, if not all, visions of God.

I.24 क्लेश कर्म विपाकाशयैरपरामृष्टः पुरुष विशेष ईश्वरः

kleśa karma vipāka āśayaih aparāmṛṣṭah puruṣa viśeṣah Īśvarah

"obstruction, action, fruition, receptacle/reservoir, unaffected, puruṣa, special, Īśvara"

In this sūtra, Patañjali starts by saying that Īśvara is a special puruṣa, and is unaffected by the obstacles to the practice (kleśas, which will be discussed in II.1 – II.11), karma (karma means 'action' and will be discussed in II.12-II.14), the results of karma, and saṃskāras (which are denoted by 'receptacle/reservoir' and will be discussed later). These four things are how Patañjali says that Īśvara is special, since the rest of us are subject to all of them.

In both Sāṃkhya and Patañjali, there are two entities that always exist: the puruṣas and prakṛti. In the Sāṃkhya Karika, ĪśvaraKṛṣṇa (the author) doesn't mention Īśvara at all, which is why many people say that Sāṃkhya is a non-theistic philosophy. Lots of commentators, and others, talk about theistic Sāṃkhya, but I've never seen a copy of this. There's also the thought that since Kṛṣṇa talks about Sāṃkhya in the Bhagavad Gītā, this is proof of a theistic Sāṃkhya. I think that's a reasonable, but not necessary, conclusion: Kṛṣṇa could be talking about a non-theistic philosophy in the very theistic Bhagavad Gītā. But whether there's a theistic Sāṃkhya is not the topic of this text. I only mention Sāṃkhya because Patañjali's philosophy is based on it. The important thing is that Īśvara, to Patañjali, is not specified as a creative divinity; however, Patañjali doesn't specify that it's not either, but Īśvara creating prakṛti and puruṣa would invalidate the requirement that they have always existed. Īśvara is just specified as a special puruṣa.

I.25 तत्र निरतिशयं सर्वज्ञ बीजम्

tatra niratiśayaṃ sarvajña bījam
"there, unsurpassed, omniscience, seed"

In I.25 Patañjali says that Īśvara is omniscient (common in most religions) and that omniscience in Īśvara is unsurpassed. This seems a little strange since omniscience means that you know everything, so why would he say that Īśvara's omniscience is unsurpassed? Bryant, in his comments on III.49, offers the idea that we, as regular puruṣas attached to a prakṛtic body and mind, can only become omniscient in terms of prakṛti, whereas Īśvara is also omniscient about things beyond prakṛti.

I.26 पूर्वेशामपि गुरुः कालेनानवच्छेदात्

pūrveśām api guruḥ kālena anavacchedāt
"of the former/ancients, even, teacher, time, not limited by"

Here Patañjali says that Īśvara is unaffected (not limited) by time. In other words, Īśvara is eternal, another common attribute of the highest entity in any religion.

He also says that, since Īśvara's eternal, Īśvara could be, and was, the teacher of the ancient seers, revealing to them absolutely correct knowledge. This is important since many of the ancient texts are believed to be revealed knowledge by Īśvara to the ancient seers during meditation. These texts are called 'śruti': 'that which was heard'. Other texts which are not considered revealed knowledge are called 'smṛti': that which is remembered.

I.27 तस्य वाचकः प्रणवः

tasya vācakaḥ praṇavaḥ
"his, designator/indicator, OM"

Patañjali says here that Īśvara's designator is OM. I have seen commentators say that OM is Īśvara's name, or something else like that, but this is not correct. The word means the divine, but is not the name of the divine. Vyāsa says that the word OM (pranava) 'is' Īśvara. Bhārati says that there are some sounds, including OM, that have the same meaning over all incarnations of the universe. According to Hinduism, the divine continually creates and destroys the universe, and this is discussed in the Bhagavad Gītā.

I.28 तज्जपस्तदर्थ भावनम्

tad japaḥ tad artha bhāvanam
"its, repetition, its, meaning, contemplating on"

Here he continues his discussion of OM and says that you should do japa on it (repeating OM over and over) and you should think about and absorb the meaning of OM. In the Ramanand Sagar version of the Rāmāyaṇa (the story of Rāma and Sītā), Hanūmān first appears just sitting on a rock in a field, chanting OM. Patañjali continues his discussion on OM in the next sūtra.

I.29 ततः प्रत्यक् चेतनाधिगमोऽप्यन्तरायाभावश्च

tataḥ pratyak cetanā adhigamaḥ api antarāya abhāvaḥ ca
"then, inner, consciousness, realization, too, obstacles, absence, also"

Here Patañjali says what happens if you repeat and meditate on OM. He says that you will get knowledge of 'the inner conscious one', the puruṣa, since that's the only thing that's conscious. So by meditating on Īśvara you get to know your own puruṣa, and that the disturbances/obstacles/obstructions, which he talks about in the next sūtra, are removed.

Vyāsa says that Īśvara is pure, blissful, free from prakṛti and the concomitant results of karma. Doing japa on OM will give you the knowledge that your puruṣa is also pure, blissful, and when you attain mokṣa, free from prakṛti and therefore free from the results of karma.

I.30 व्याधि स्त्यान संशय प्रमादालस्याविरति भ्रान्ति दर्शनालब्ध भूमिकत्वानवस्थितत्वानि चित्त विक्षेपास्तेऽन्तरायाः

vyādhi styāna saṃśaya pramāda ālasya avirati bhrānti darśana alabdha bhūmikatva anavasthitatvāni citta vikṣepāḥ te antarāyāḥ

"disease, laziness, doubt, carelessness, sloth, lack of dispassion, confusion, of philosophies/belief-systems, failing to obtain, ground, instability, mind, distractions, they, obstacles"

In I.30 he lists the 9 antarāyas (obstacles/disturbances/obstructions). Bryant likes the word disturbances because he says that the kleśas are usually called obstacles or obstructions and he thinks using either of those two words confuses things. I will just use the word antarāya to get around that issue. The antarāyas are disease, idleness, doubt, carelessness, sloth, lack of dispassion/non-attachment, confusion of philosophies/belief-systems, failure to attain a ground for meditation, and failure to keep the ground. All of the antarāyas will keep you from diligently following the path; for example, it's hard to meditate when you are sick because you may be in pain.

The word darśana has a number of meanings, e.g. vision, view, belief system, philosophy (as in the six darśanas of which Patañjali is one). Here he means philosophy. Confusion of philosophies (or belief systems) is when you don't understand correctly what Patañjali is saying, or you are interpreting what he said to match your different philosophy, both of which can cause you to go in the wrong direction.

Lack of dispassion says that you haven't mastered vairāgya, or non-attachment (see I.15, I.16). It also means engaging in sexuality, which can be a real distraction to your sādhana.

The last two items in the list are failure to attain a ground for meditation, which implies that you haven't fully made your sādhana part of your life, and failure to keep the ground, which implies that even though you may have made your sādhana part of your life, you have fallen off the path and let it stop being a part of your life.

I.31 दुःख दौर्मनस्याङ्गमेजयत्व श्वास प्रश्वासा विक्षेप सह भुवः

duḥkha daurmanasya aṅgam ejayatva śvāsa prasvāsāḥ vikṣepa saha bhu-
  vaḥ

"pain, dejection, limbs, trembling, inhalation, exhalation, obstacles, accompany"

I.31 lists some other problems that accompany the antarāyas. These are pain/suffering, dejection/frustration/anguish, trembling/unsteadiness of the limbs, inhalation, and exhalation. There are three kinds of pain: within oneself, caused by others, and caused by deities or natural forces. Vācaspati Miśra, a well known commentator, gives examples of these: 1) within oneself is disease or mental pain from unsatisfied desires, 2) from others such as being mauled by a tiger, and 3) natural forces such as planetary influences. Trembling of the limbs means that you can't sit still in meditation. The last two items in I.31, deal with involuntary or uneven inhalation and exhalation. It's hard to meditate if your breathing isn't smooth and quiet.

When I had my shoulder surgery a number of years ago, I still sat and attempted to meditate even though it hurt most every night for a few months. In the book "Cave in the Snow" by Vicki MacKenzie, the Buddhist meditator Tenzin Palmo was living alone up in the Himalayas for 11 years. At one point she got an eye infection, so she meditated on the pain for a month until it got better. So it's possible to work through these problems.

I.32 तत्प्रतिषेधार्थमेक तत्त्वाभ्यासः

tat pratiṣedha artham eka tattva abhyāsaḥ

"that, driving away, purpose, one, real element, practice"

Here Patañjali says that you should meditate on a single object to eliminate (drive away) the antarāyas and the accompanying problems. The definition of the word 'tattva' is principle/factor/reality/real element/object. Hariharānanda says that some commentators think that 'principle' means Īśvara only. He says, however, if that was true Patañjali wouldn't have used the phrase 'one principle' but would have used Īśvara. He goes on to say that if he meant only Īśvara he wouldn't have needed this sūtra because that's covered in the previous sūtra. Therefore, he says that you should meditate on only one object, whatever that object is.

In his commentary on this sūtra, Vyāsa says that the antarāyas, which are opposing meditation, can be checked and overcome by abhyāsa/practice and vairāgya/non-attachment (from I.12 – I.16). He says that if your mind gets disturbed you need to use these two things to fix the problem.

Section Summary

This is the end of Patañjali's discussion of how to get to samādhi. To summarize, you can get into samādhi by your nature (videhās and prakṛti-layas in I.19), or by faith in the practice, vigor, memory, samādhi, and discernment (I.20), or by Īśvara praṇidhāna (I.23). You use abhyāsa and vairāgyam to do this. He also gives his definition of Īśvara and then discusses the obstacles to getting to samādhi.

I.33 – I.40 Purifying the Mind

The next set of sūtras in Patañjali is sūtras I.33 – I.39 which discuss how to purify the mind and get mental stability/equilibrium. He also gives some ideas on what to do, or what to meditate on to do so.

I.33 मैत्री करुणा मुदितोपेक्षाणां सुख दुःख पुण्यापुण्य विषयाणां

भावनातश्चित्त प्रसादनम्

maitrī karuṇā mudita upekṣāṇāṃ sukha duḥkha puṇya apuṇya
    viṣayāṇāṃ bhāvanātaḥ citta prasādanam
"friendly, compassion, joyful, indifference, happy, suffering, virtuous,
    non-virtuous, with regard to, from the attitude, mind, purifying"

In this sūtra Patañjali gives some instruction on how to purify your mind and keep your mental equanimity. He says "by being friendly to the happy, compassionate to the miserable, joyful to the virtuous, and indifferent to the non-virtuous, the mind is purified and becomes serene. The first three items in the list are not difficult for most people. The fourth one, disregard/indifference to the non-virtuous/wicked, is a bit more problematic. This doesn't mean that you should ignore non-virtuous people; it means that you don't let yourself get caught up in their stuff. If someone is breaking the law, it's ok to put them in jail, but don't let your mind become disturbed by them.

The important point to this sūtra is that having these four attitudes towards these four different types of people is an option to purify your mind, which leads to mental stability. The mind has the qualities of the guṇas, tamas (ignorance/inactivity), rajas (activity), and sattva (calmness). Here, Patañjali wants you to remove as much of the tamas and rajas as you can so that only sattva is left, which is what he means by purifying your mind. It's much easier to meditate when your citta(mind) is very sattvic. Tamas will make you want to sleep, rajas will keep your mind from settling down to meditate, but sattva is good for meditation due to the stable calmness from sattva. A pure mind leads to mental stability/equilibrium so that your mind doesn't continually go from happiness to unhappiness, i.e. stays in a state of bliss, and doesn't wander during meditation.

I.34 प्रच्छर्दन विधारणाभ्यां वा प्राणस्य

pracchardana vidhāraṇābhyāṃ vā prāṇasya
"exhalation, restraint from both, or, of the breath"

In this sūtra he says that controlling the breath will help keep your mind serene. I have found that doing prāṇāyāma ('breath control', see II.49 – II.51) immediately followed by meditation tends to make the meditation better, because both the ida and piṅgala nadīs tend to both be open, and the sleepy nadī (Iḍā) balances out the 'monkey mind' nadī (piṅgala). While Patañjali doesn't specifically use the word prāṇāyāma here, it is his definition of prāṇāyāma in II.49.

I.35 विषय वती वा प्रवृत्तिरुत्पन्ना मनसः स्थिति निबन्धनी

viṣaya vatī vā pravṛttiḥ utpannā manasaḥ sthiti nibandhanī
"sense objects, having, or, inclination/activity, arises, manas, steadiness,
   firmly establishes"

In I.35 – I.39 Patañjali gives several examples of things that you can meditate on to get mental stability. Here Patañjali says that by meditating on sense objects an inclination to meditate arises, and by meditating you can get mental equilibrium. In other words, the more you do it, the more you want to do it. He also says that meditating firmly establishes the steadiness of the manas (the part of the mind that interfaces with the senses). Bhārati (aka Pandit Uṣarbudh Arya), according to Zambito, translated this one as "The natural mental tendency of concentrating (even) on an object of senses, when developed, stills and purifies the mind."

Vyāsa and many of the other commentators translate utpannā as 'higher activity' and talk about getting super-normal sense impressions by meditating on specific sense organs in the body, e.g. the tip of the tongue – you get super-normal taste. Vyāsa also says that you can get super-normal sense impressions from meditating on the sun, moon, planets, etc., and that from the siddhis/super-normal powers, discussed in the third chapter, which you get from meditation, your doubts will be removed and your mind will become steady.

I.36 विशोका वा ज्योतिष्मती

viśokā vā jyotiṣmatī

"free of pain, or, luminous"

Or you can get mental equilibrium from meditation on something that is pain free or luminous. Anything that is pain free and luminous has very little, if any, rajas and tamas, and is full of sattva. The buddhi and the ahaṃkāra are very sattvic and therefore qualify as being pain free and luminous. Vyāsa suggests meditating on the lotus cakra in the heart.

I.37 वीत राग विषयं वा चित्तम्

vīta rāga viṣayaṃ vā cittam

"without, desire, objects, or, mind"

Or you can get mental equilibrium by meditating on those people whose minds are free of desires. Those people are your guru, ancient sages/ṛṣis, etc. If you meditate on these people, Patañjali says that their serene quality becomes your own and you get mental equilibrium. In Patañjali's definition of samādhi in III.3, he says that in that state, the object of meditation is the only thing in your mind, so the idea is that, if your guru has a mind free of desire, that serenity becomes yours too. If you are lucky enough to have a guru, you can meditate on them. If not, you can meditate on one of the ancient sages/ṛṣis who calls to you.

So how do you determine if a person is a real guru? After all, you can't just go down to the local Rent-A-Guru store. Aside from the ways to know if one is a fake, mentioned below, Bryant quotes the Bhagavad Gītā, II.54 and XIV.21-27. In these ślokas, Arjuna asks Kṛṣṇa how do you know if a person is one of steady wisdom, i.e. a true guru. Kṛṣṇa says that when a person is satisfied in the self by means of the self. He has renounced all desires, is not agitated in misfortune, and whose desires are gone. Kṛṣṇa says in the XIV.21-27 that a person that has transcended the guṇas (a real guru) is completely detached (see Patañjali I.15-16), is the same in pain and pleasure, to whom gold, a stone, and a lump of dirt are the same, and who treats all people the same. I paraphrased these ślokas, but you can go and read them in their entirety.

If a teacher doesn't meet these requirements, you should keep looking. There's a saying that when the student is ready the guru appears, and when the guru is ready the student appears.

Bryant makes a very important point here about fake gurus. The problem is how to know if someone is a real guru or a fake. He discusses that the many fake gurus and the associated sexual issues and other scandals that they've had are a real problem these days. There are many charismatic 'gurus' out there who are not real gurus. I tell my students all the time that real gurus can be hard to find because they are hiding and doing their sādhana. If you find someone who says "I'm a guru", run away. They aren't real. If you find someone who says that you can only study with them and nobody else (I've run into a few people whose teacher says that), run away. They aren't real either. If you are required to give them money, run away. Fake gurus don't have minds without desires, so you can't get the serene quality you are after by meditating on them.

My teacher has never asked me for anything. One time when I stopped by with some questions she said that I drove her crazy with my questions, but that she knew that I really wanted the answers, so she would spend the time to answer them. She once told me that her guru told her to go study with anyone she wanted; if she still had questions after that he would answer them for her.

I.38 स्वप्र निद्रा ज्ञानालम्बनं वा

svapna nidrā jñāna ālambanaṃ vā
"dream, sleep, knowledge, support, or"

Or you can get mental equilibrium by meditating on the knowledge from dreams or sleep. There is a difference of opinion here. Some commentators say that you meditate on the knowledge of the dream state. Some say that you meditate on knowledge that you've received from dreams. Some say that you meditate on the images of dreams or the state of dreamless sleep. Patañjali doesn't specify what he means here, and Vyāsa doesn't say much either. So this is a confusing one, and it's not clear which, if any, of the options above is what Patañjali meant.

I.39 यथाभिमत ध्यानाद्वा

yathā abhimata dhyānāt vā
"as, desired, by meditation on, or"

Or you can get mental equilibrium by meditating on anything you want. I like this one. After giving you several options of what to meditate on, he says that if none of those work you can meditate on anything you want. The caveat here is that, whatever you meditate on, it must be static (unchanging). If you 'meditate' on walking on a beach, that isn't meditation because your mind will be moving as you visualize walking down the beach.

I.40 परमाणु परम महत्त्वान्तोऽस्य वशीकारः

parama aṇu parama mahattva antaḥ asya vaśīkāraḥ
"greatest, insignificantly small, greatest, magnitude, up to, his, mastery"

Here he says that the yogī's mastery extends from meditating on very smallest of things, up to the entire universe. He's giving us an idea of what an advanced yogī can do. It's a continuation of the previous sūtra where he says that you can meditate on anything you want. You can meditate on the smallest part of matter up to the entire universe.

A point needs to be made here. 'Aṇu', is usually translated as atom, but it doesn't exactly mean atom. It means the very smallest thing, so as science knows about things smaller than atoms, what it indicates changes, but the word stays the same.

Section Summary

In summary, in these sūtras he says how to get mental equilibrium by using four attitudes towards four types of people, by doing prāṇāyāma, and by meditation on sense objects. He also adds that meditation purifies your mind and gives some suggestions on what you can meditate on.

I.17, I.18, and I.41 – I.51 Samādhi

To summarize the earlier parts of the first chapter, in I.1 Patañjali said that he's going to talk about yoga. In I.2 he said what the state of yoga is. I.3 gives what the goal of yoga is. I.4 – I.16 discuss the vṛttis and how to get rid of them. In I.17 and I.18 he gives some introductory definitions of the two major types of samādhi. In I.19 – I.32 he gives how to get to samādhi, whether by the methods in I.12 – I.16 or by Īśvara praṇidhāna. From I.33 – I.40 he gives some options of what you can meditate on to get samādhi.

The rest of the chapter discusses the various levels of samādhi and how to attain mokṣa. <u>Patañjali's idea is that you need to meditate on the right thing for each level of samādhi until you truly understand the difference between puruṣa and prakṛti.</u> This section is a bit difficult, so take your time to understand it.

I.17 वितर्क विचारानन्दास्मिता रूपानुगमात् संप्रज्ञातः

vitarka vicāra ānanda asmitā rūpa anugamāt samprajñātaḥ

"vitarka, vicāra, ānanda, asmitā, form, accompanied by, samprajñāta"

<u>Here Patañjali defines one of the two major types of samādhi: samprajñāta. He discusses the other type, asamprajñāta, in the next sūtra, I.18. Samprajñāta samādhi is when you are meditating on an object, a seed, so this kind of samādhi is also known as 'with seed' or sabīja.</u> There are four levels to samprajñāta, and I have left them untranslated because they are complicated and the definitions are long, and these are words you should know. I have also left samprajñāta untranslated for the same reason.

The four levels of samprajñāta are

vitarka = with words, meaning, and ideas on physical/gross matter
vicāra = with words, meaning, and ideas on subtle matter
ānanda = with bliss
asmitā = with the thought of 'I'

I will discuss these levels in more detail later in this section, but briefly what you do in samprajñāta samādhi is meditate on the right thing for each level until you truly understand the difference between puruṣa and prakṛti in order to attain mokṣa.

I.18 विराम प्रत्ययाभ्यास पूर्वः संस्कार शेषोऽन्यः

virāma pratyaya abhyāsa pūrvaḥ saṃskāra śeṣaḥ anyaḥ
"cessation, thought, practice, previous, mental imprint, remainder, the
other"

Patañjali says here that the other samādhi, asamprajñāta, is preceded by practice/abhyāsa and has only latent saṃskāras remaining. Saṃskāras are mental impressions created with every vṛtti you have. They cause you to tend to respond the same way to the same mental input. I like to think of them as ruts, depressions made by wheels in mud. As part of your sādhana you need to 'fill in' old ruts that are kliṣṭa, that keep you from moving forward in your sādhana, and create new ones that help keep you on the path, akliṣṭa. The idea is that after awhile, you will only have good ruts and will have filled in all the unhelpful ones.

To understand I.17 and I.18 you need to understand the Sāṃkhya devolution tree, which you can find in just about any book on Sāṃkhya, and also in most commentaries on Patañjali. See appendix F in this book. I discussed this briefly in the introduction to this text, but I will give a short summary of this again as it's critical to understanding these sūtras. According to Sāṃkhya, which Patañjali accepts, creation came about when puruṣa and prakṛti came together. The first devolute from this was buddhi, the discriminating part of the mind, which decides which things presented to it are either good or bad, useful or useless, to the person. From buddhi came ahaṃkāra, the ego, which is the sense of an "I" as separate from "you". Out of that came a number of things: the powers of the 10 indriyas (instruments/senses) of knowledge/jñāna (eyes, ears, etc.) and action/karma (hands, feet, etc.). Also you get the manas, which is the connection to the senses and the outside world. It brings in sense objects, determines what they are, categorizes them, and presents them to the buddhi. Out of ahaṃkāra also comes the subtle elements (tanmātras) and out of the tanmātras comes the mahā bhūtas or gross elements.

Once you get to samādhi, after getting past dhāraṇā (concentration) and into dhyāna (meditation) (see III.1 – III.3), then you can use samādhi to work on how you get to truly understand your true self, puruṣa, and attain mokṣa to stop suffering (II.15 – II. 28). When we start, as yogīs, to meditate, we need something to fix our minds on, an object or seed. This is something in gross matter, and is at the end of the devolution tree. In samādhi, there is only the object of meditation – not an I or the act of meditating (III.3). Your mind is still for as long as you want, i.e. for as long as you are meditating. This is the vitarka level of samprajñāta samādhi in I.17. It's meditation with words on the object of meditation and means that you understand and look at the object of meditation with words.

At some point you will completely understand the object and will find it not satisfying and will want to move deeper. Then you will meditate on the cause of the object, i.e. subtle matter, and you are now in the vicāra level of samprajñāta samādhi. Again, you will finally understand everything about your object and find it unsatisfying.

Then you move to the cause of subtle matter, the ahaṃkāra, and you are in the ānanda level of samprajñāta samādhi. You will finally understand everything about the ahaṃkāra and again be unsatisfied.

Next you move on to meditating on buddhi, and you are in the asmitā level of samprajñāta samādhi. When you truly understand buddhi, you will know that it comes from the conjunction, or coming together, of puruṣa and prakṛti. When you truly understand this, you know pretty much everything that needs to be known, III.49 and IV.31, and get ṛtambharā, the truth bearing wisdom mentioned in I.48, and can finally move to asamprajñāta samādhi and attain mokṣa.

One question that I asked my teacher was, if my mind is not moving, how am I supposed to get the viveka khyātiḥ, discriminative wisdom, that I'm supposed to be getting from samādhi? She said that it was an excellent question and gave me the metaphor of the still pond. Assume that the knowledge that we are looking for is at the bottom of the pond, and you are sitting in a boat in the middle of the pond. If there is any wind, i.e. fluctuations in your mind, there are ripples in the water and you can't see the bottom. If, however, there is no wind, i.e. your mind is still in samādhi, then you can get this wisdom. I asked, "but how do I get it if my mind is not moving?" She said that the wisdom just appears in your mind and you just know it. She calls it the 'aha moment'. This is what I've experienced. When I have come out of meditation, I sometimes have knowledge that I didn't have before.

Above, Patañjali gave definitions of the two major types of samādhi, and I gave some introductory information on what goes on in samādhi. In the next set of sūtras, Patañjali discusses in detail the levels of samādhi, what happens, and how you get to asamprajñāta samādhi, and then attain mokṣa.

I.41 क्षीण वृत्तेरभिजात्स्येव मनेर्ग्रहितृ ग्रहण ग्राह्येषु तत्स्थ तदञ्जनता समापत्तिः

kṣīṇa vṛtteḥ abhijātsya iva maneḥ grahitṛ grahaṇa grāhyeṣu tat stha tat
    añjanatā samāpattiḥ
"weakened, fluctuations/vṛttis, nobly born, like, crystal, knower, instru-
    ment of knowing, object of knowledge, that, stable, that, identity, as-
    suming an original form, samādhi"

In this sūtra, Patañjali is defining samādhi in a precise way, and not
involving the layers that he mentioned in I.17, or the lack of layers in I.18.
An important point to remember is that the puruṣa doesn't meditate, only the
buddhi does, because the puruṣa never changes; it's a silent witness to what
is going on in the buddhi.

In this sūtra, Patañjali uses the word abhijātsya, which means born/
produced/nobly-born, in an unusual way: he uses it to mean transparent.

This sūtra is a different way of defining samādhi than in III.3. In I.41
Patañjali says that samprajñāta samādhi is when the mind has no vṛttis, i.e. is
not fluctuating, it becomes just like a transparent jewel, taking the color of
whatever it's placed on, whether the object is the knower, the instrument of
knowledge, or the object of knowledge. The knower is the buddhi, the
instrument of knowledge is the senses, and the object of knowledge is any
gross or subtle object. In III.3 he says that in samādhi the idea of 'I am
meditating on that' is lost and only 'that' is left. The idea here is that, in
samādhi, the entire buddhi is filled with the object of meditation and nothing
else, not even the idea of 'I am meditating' exists in the buddhi.

When he says that the buddhi reflects the object of meditation like a
gem or crystal, he's saying that in samprajñāta samādhi the buddhi takes the
form of, or is colored by, the object of meditation; if you put a pure crystal on
a blue cloth, it looks blue, but if you put it on a red cloth, it looks red. So
your buddhi 'is colored by' the object.

Remember that you can meditate on subtle matter such as the buddhi
and the ahaṃkāra, so it makes sense that you can meditate on the knower as
well as the instrument of knowledge. See the discussion in I.18 above.

Here Patañjali introduces a new term, samāpatti, which is a synonym for samādhi. I have checked numerous commentators, and there's no general agreement on this. However, half of them either say that these two terms are the same or don't even comment on the difference (see appendix G for a discussion of this). The others don't agree on what the difference is. So I think that Patañjali just used a different word here to keep his text interesting.

I.42 तत्र शब्दार्थ ज्ञान विकल्पै: संकीर्णा सवितर्का समापत्ति:

tatra śabda artha jñāna vikalpaiḥ saṃkīrṇā savitarkā samāpattiḥ

"there, word, meaning, knowledge, with options, mixed, savitarkā, samādhi"

In I.42 – I.44 he's adding two different levels to the four he already gave in I.17 in his description of samprajñāta samādhi. Those layers were vitarka, vicāra, ānanda, and asmitā. Please note that in I.17 he left out the prefix 'sa' for each of the four layers. 'Sa' as a prefix means 'with', so savitarka means 'with vitarkā'.

Here he actually gives the definition of 'vitarka' from I.17: it's samādhi on physical/gross objects with words, meaning, and ideas. For example, if I say 'horse' you immediately link the word to your mental picture (meaning) of a large four-footed mammal, and you have ideas on horses from previous interactions with horses. So if you meditate on 'horse' these three things are part of what you are meditating on and they affect the meditation, but not necessarily in a bad way. It's just that this level of samādhi involves these three things. These three things are not part of the next level, and the next sūtra discusses this.

I.43 स्मृति परिशुद्धौ स्व रुप शून्ये इव अर्थ मात्र निर्भासा निर्वितर्का

smṛti pariśuddhau sva rūpa śūnyā iva artha mātra nirbhāsā nirvitarkā
"memory, upon purification, own, nature, empty/nothing, like, object,
   only, shining forth, nirvitarka"

Here he gives the definition of the first of the two new levels: nirvitarka. Nirvitarka means without (nir) words, meaning, and ideas (vitarka). He says that when the memory is purified, the mind is empty of its own nature, and the object of meditation only is shining through, this is nirvitarka. In this level, memory is turned off, and the mind contains only the vision of the object without figuring out what it is from words, meaning, and memory. The mind is looking at the object – horse, and noting the number of legs, the tail, color, etc. It doesn't know that it's a horse, or remember any previous inter-actions or knowledge of horses.

I.44 एतयैव सविचारा निर्विचारा च सूक्ष्म विषया व्याख्याता

etayā eva savicārā nirvicārā ca sūkṣma viṣayā vyākhyātā
"by this, also, savicāra, nirvicāra, and, subtle, objects, are explained"

Here he says that savicāra (with words, meaning, and ideas) and nirvicāra (without words, meaning, and ideas) on subtle objects/matter, are explained the same way. The difference is that in these two levels you are meditating on the tanmātras (one type of subtle matter): sound, touch, form, taste, and smell. If you remember the Sāṃkhya devolution tree, the tanmātras devolve into gross matter (the mahā bhūtas): space, wind, fire, water, and earth. All gross, physical objects are made up of combinations of the mahā bhūtas. So here, in savicāra samādhi you are meditating on the tanmātras with words, meaning, and ideas. He also says that nirvicāra samādhi is meditation on the tanmātras without words, meaning, or ideas.

I.45 सूक्ष्म विषयत्वं चालिङ्ग पर्यवसानम्

sūkṣma viṣayatvaṃ ca aliṅga paryavasānam

"subtle, having for as objects, and, without a mark, termination"

Patañjali continues I.44 with I.45 "subtle matter extends up to pradhāna." In the Sāṃkhya devolution tree (Appendix F), you start with pradhāna, or undifferentiated/primordial prakṛti. The first devolute is buddhi, which then devolves into the ahaṃkāra, which devolves into the tanmātras which finally devolve into gross matter. So here he's saying that as you continue in your samprajñāta samādhi you continue to move up the devolution tree, meditating on more and more subtle things until you get to pradhāna, and then you can't go any farther. Since pradhāna is the starting point, an ontological entity, this makes sense.

After you have finished meditating on the tanmātras in savicāra and nirvicāra samādhi, then you move up to meditating on the ahaṃkāra (sa-ānanda samādhi). When you understand ahaṃkāra, you realize it's not satisfying and move up to meditating on the buddhi (sa-asmitā samādhi). Remember that ānanda and asmitā samādhi are the last two levels of samprajñāta samādhi in I.17; the prefix 'sa' as mentioned before means 'with'. Patañjali never mentions these last two levels other than in I.17, but some of the commentators say that they both apply to the first two levels of prakṛti after pradhāna, i.e. buddhi and ahaṃkāra. See Appendix E for my thoughts on this.

I.46 ता एव सबीजः समाधिः

tāḥ eva sabījaḥ samādhiḥ

"they, only, with seed, samādhi"

The Saṃskṛtaṃ word for 'with seed' means that you are meditating on an object, i.e. samprajñāta samādhi. <u>Remember that the difference between samprajñāta and asamprajñāta samādhi is that the former is 'with seed' and the latter is 'without seed'.</u> Patañjali is saying that I.41 – I.45 are talking about samprajñāta samādhi.

I.47 निर्विचार वैशारद्येऽध्यात्म प्रसादः

nirvicāra vaiśāradye adhyātma prasādaḥ
"nirvicāra, proficiency, self, purity/clearness/clarity"

Here, Patañjali says that you get the knowledge of your self (puruṣa) when you have mastered nirvicāra samādhi. According to the philosophy, the buddhi can't directly perceive anything that is more subtle than itself. The only things that are more subtle than buddhi are puruṣa and pradhāna (primordial prakṛti). So the buddhi gets an indirect perception/knowledge of these two items.

According to Bryant, Vijñānabhikṣu says here that when you get proficiency in nirvicāra you get discriminating wisdom with regard to prakṛti and puruṣa. Remember that knowledge of the difference between puruṣa and prakṛti is the viveka khyatiḥ (discriminative wisdom) that we need to attain mokṣa.

I.48 ऋतं भरा तत्र प्रज्ञा

ṛtaṃ bharā tatra prajñā
'truth, bearing, there, wisdom"

Here, Patañjali is expanding on the knowledge that you get in nirvicāra samādhi from the previous sūtra in which he said that you get knowledge of the puruṣa. This sūtra says that that knowledge is perfect truth. There is no trace of false or incorrect knowledge at this point.

The question can be asked: how do you get this knowledge from samādhi since your mind isn't moving? The answer is that this knowledge just appears in your mind when you come out of samādhi.

Another interesting question is how this knowledge fits into the three valid sources of right knowledge, pramāṇa, from I.7, since there doesn't seem to be any direct sensory perception in samādhi. Bryant, in his discussion of the next sūtra, mentions that this knowledge is a form of direct perception, pratyakṣa, but it's not regular sense perception, but transcends normal sense perception.

I.49 श्रुतानुमान प्रज्ञाभ्यामन्य विषया विशेषार्थत्वात्

śruta anumāna prajñābhyām anya viṣayā viśeṣa arthatvāt
"heard, inference, wisdom from both (heard and inference), other, object, specific, as its object"

Here he's saying that ṛtam (mentioned in the previous sūtra and translated as "truth") is different than what you get from testimony (heard) and inference because those two pramāṇas, are about generalities, whereas ṛtam, a form of direct/sensory perception, is about specifics, e.g. the specific horse you are meditating on. However, ṛtam is different from direct sensory perception since that can only give you information about gross matter, and ṛtam is about more subtle things, i.e. puruṣa and prakṛti. In I.47 he said that you get ṛtam once you master nirvicāra samādhi, and in I.48 he said that it's true knowledge.

Remember from I.7 that the three sources of correct information (pramāṇas) are sensory perception, inference, and testimony.

I.50 तज्जः संस्कारोऽन्य संस्कार प्रतिबन्धी

tat jaḥ saṃskāraḥ anya saṃskāra pratibandhī
"that, produced, mental impression, other, mental impressions, opposes/obstructs"

Here Patañjali is saying that the saṃskāras you get from truth bearing wisdom (ṛtam) acquired in nirvicāra samādhi oppose and destroy all other saṃskāras. The other saṃskāras are ones that take your mind back into gross matter and keep you from attaining mokṣa. So you are getting new saṃskāras that keep you going in the right direction, and none that point you in the wrong direction. At this point you are at the highest level of samprajñāta samādhi, getting ready for asamprajñāta samādhi and mokṣa.

I.51 तस्यापि निरोधे सर्व निरोधान्निर्बीजः समाधिः

tasya api nirodhe sarva nirodhāt nirbījaḥ samādhiḥ
"Of that, even, upon cessation, all, from the cessation, seedless,
   samādhi"

Patañjali says that when you get rid of even those last saṃskāras, from the ṛtam acquired in nirvicāra samādhi, you get nirbīja samādhi (seedless samādhi). Nirbīja samādhi is the same as asamprajñāta samādhi. Vyāsa makes this clear in his commentary on I.18, which is the definition of asamprajñāta samādhi: एष निर्बीजः समाधिरसंप्रज्ञातः "This nirbīja samādhi is asamprajñāta".

After you get the new saṃskāras from I.50, you are trying to get rid of even those new saṃskāras, and are still in samprajñāta samādhi. Once you get rid of even those saṃskāras, as Patañjali says in this sūtra, you attain asamprajñāta samādhi, at which time your mind permanently disconnects from your puruṣa, and you have attained mokṣa, which is the goal of yoga, as mentioned in I.3.

At this point, after the mind disconnects from your puruṣa, you don't have a body. This supports the idea of mahā samādhi, where the yogī goes into samādhi, and purposely never comes back; otherwise the yogī would have to wait until death to get mokṣa.

This is the end of the first chapter of Patañjali, the chapter on samādhi.

Section Summary

In this section Patañjali discusses the various levels of samprajñāta samādhi, and in the last sūtra very briefly discusses asamprajñāta samādhi, the goal of yoga. Patañjali is inconsistent in defining the levels of samādhi and how they fit together: see Appendix E for more information. However, I think that we can safely say that you have to go through some number of levels of samprajñāta samādhi, to get to asamprajñāta samādhi and then attain mokṣa. So while the details are not clear, the overall intent is clear.

<u>Chapter Summary</u>

In this chapter Patañjali introduces the topic of the text, yoga, defines yoga as the stilling of the fluctuations of the mind, and defines the goal of yoga, mokṣa, as the puruṣa (your true self) being separated from your prakṛtic (your body/mind complex), and being in a state of complete aloneness forever. He then discusses how to stop the fluctuations of the mind (through practice and non-attachment). Then he defines samādhi as the tool used to attain mokṣa, and discusses the three ways to get to samādhi: being born after being a videhā or a prakṛti-laya (very advanced yogis), working at it, or surrendering to Īśvara (the divine). Next, he discusses how to purify your mind so you can get into samādhi. Finally, he finishes the chapter by discussing the various levels of samādhi, and how you attain mokṣa from samādhi.

Sādhana Pāda

II.1 – II.11 Kriyā Yoga and Kleśas

The first chapter was about samādhi, and while it gives information about samādhi to everyone, it's mostly aimed at highly advanced yogīs that can actually get into samādhi. The second chapter, the "Sādhana Pāda" is more of a cookbook for all the rest of us that are either just starting on our journey, or those of us that have been on it for awhile but aren't highly advanced. Kleśas (II.3 – II.11) are impediments/obstacles/afflictions to attaining mokṣa. There are five of them. In II.1 and II.2 he gives some introductory information on them. In II.12 – II.14 he discusses karma and how it affects us in the current life and in future lives. In II.15-II.28 he discusses why we should take up yoga and high level information about what we're trying to do and where we're going. In II.29 – II.55 he introduces the first five of the eight limbs (angas) of his classical Aṣṭāṅga Yoga, which is not to be confused with Aṣṭāṅga Vinyasa Yoga as taught by Pattabhi Jois. The last three are discussed in chapter three. The eight limbs are

2. yama – ethical restraints
3. niyama – observances and attitudes
4. āsana – postures
5. prāṇāyāma – increasing/expanding prāṇa in the body
6. pratyāhāra – withdrawing from the senses
7. dhāraṇā – concentration
8. dhyāna – meditation
9. samādhi – tool for getting discriminative wisdom (viveka khyātiḥ) while in meditation

II.1 तपः स्वाध्यायेश्वर प्रणिधानानि क्रिया योगः

tapaḥ, svādhyāya, Īśvara, praṇidhānāni, kriyā, yogaḥ
"heat/effort/austerity, study, surrender to the Lord (Īśvara), action, yoga"

Here, Patañjali says that kriyā yoga (the yoga of action), consists of three things: tapas (effort/austerity), svādhyāya (study), and Īśvara praṇidhāna (surrender to Īśvara). These are what a brand new yogī is told to do to get on the yogic path, so as not to not overwhelm a new yogī with rules and requirements. Kriyā yoga is also a good framework for a householder to practice yoga since it doesn't have the restriction of brahmacharya/celibacy in the niyamas of the eight limbs of Aṣṭāṅga (II.29), as sex is generally considered a part of being married.

After the new yogī has been practicing these three things for awhile, and is ready, you give them the eight limbs of Aṣṭāṅga Yoga, which are detailed later in this chapter. Then, when the yogī becomes highly advanced the only requirement is to still the fluctuations of the citta in samādhi, which is sūtra I.2. My teacher has said that if you truly understand I.2 you don't need to read the rest of the book. Now we need to go over the three parts of kriyā yoga.

Tapas means heat/effort/asceticism in your practice. This word has been translated as "accepting pain as purification". While I can understand why it's translated this way, it really misses the point. Patañjali says that you need to put some effort in your practice (see I.13 and I.14). If you don't put effort into it, you won't get the appropriate results for a very long time. Asceticism is also meant by tapas. Asceticism means focusing exclusively on your practice. While this is a gradual process over many lifetimes, things outside of your practice will gradually fall off until the only thing left is your practice.

Asceticism also means getting rid of unnecessary stuff that you don't need, but it also means that you don't do something that you might want to do, because you want to work on your practice. For example, if you liked to go out drinking with your friends before you took up the yogic path, you might not do this anymore, or gradually not do it over time. Is this painful? Maybe, depending on how you look at it. If you want to go drinking but you have to work on your practice, then there might be some 'pain.' If, however, you don't want to go drinking because you would rather be working on your practice, then you are still doing austerity but there's no pain. There are yogīs, demons (a type of non-human in Hinduism), etc., performing severe austerities. According to one story, a demoness stood on one foot at the top of a mountain for 10,000 years to show Lord Śiva that she really wanted the boon that she was asking for.

Svādhyāya means to study. The commentators have some differing opinions on exactly what this constitutes. Vyāsa says that it means repeating mantras (japa) and studying of scripture. Others say it just means to study. I like to include any study you do to help you on your sādhana (yogic path) as included in svādhyāya.

I like to expand the definition of svādhyāya a bit, especially for yoga teachers. For them, I like to say that it is studying 'of yourself' and 'by yourself.' If you study by yourself, you can give yourself the time to figure things out so that you can bring what you learn to your students. For example, if you have pain somewhere when doing an āsana, you can stop when you are practicing by yourself to investigate how to relieve the pain. Then, when teaching a class, and a student has that same pain/discomfort, you can apply what you learned to the student to help them. Or if you have pain when meditating, you can also investigate how to relieve the pain and bring that to your students too.

Īśvara praṇidhāna is defined as surrender to Īśvara, or devotion to Īśvara. Bryant says that since it's not an option as in I.23, this shows that Patañjali requires a theistic approach to the path. Note that in I.23 Īśvara praṇidhāna is given as an alternative way to get to samādhi, which is a tool/ state of meditation where you work to get the information or discriminative wisdom (viveka khyātiḥ) that you need to attain mokṣa. This theistic approach is further elaborated in II.44 and II.45.

II.2 समाधि भावनार्थः क्लेश तनू करणार्थश्च

samādhi bhāvana arthaḥ kleśa tanū karaṇa arthaḥ ca

"samādhi, developing, purpose, obstacles, weakening, making, purpose, and"

Here Patañjali tells you why a yogī would do Kriyā Yoga: getting into samādhi and getting rid of the kleśas. The kleśas are a new term that Patañjali uses that means afflictions/obstructions/impediments. So kleśas keep you from getting into samādhi and therefore attaining mokṣa.

Next he's going to give a list of them and discuss them one-by-one.

II.3 अविद्याऽस्मिता राग द्वेषाभिनिवेशाः क्लेशाः

avidyā asmitā rāga dveṣa abhiniveśāḥ kleśāḥ

"ignorance, ego, attraction, aversion, fear-of-death/clinging-to-life,
   kleśas"

- avidyā = ignorance
- asmitā = ego,
- rāga = attraction
- dveṣa = aversion
- abhiniveśāḥ = fear-of-death/clinging-to-life

Note that there are only five kleśas, unlike vṛttis (mental fluctuations,
see I.2), where there are five types but an infinite number of them. There are
many instances of rāga/attraction and dveṣa/aversion (defined below), but
only five kleśas, and we need to get rid of all of them to attain mokṣa. We'll
go through the five kleśas in the next 6 sūtras.

II.4 अविद्या क्षेत्रं उत्तरेषां प्रसुप्त तनु विच्छिन्नोदाराणाम्

avidyā kṣetram uttareṣām prasupta tanu vicchhinna udārāṇām

"ignorance, field, of the others, dormant, weakened, interrupted, active"

Avidyā is ignorance. This is the first kleśa and Patañjali says that it's the
breeding ground of all the other kleśas, i.e. the others come out of it
(devolve). Patañjali gives some information about avidyā in this sūtra and
how it relates to the kleśas, and then in the next five sūtras explains all five
kleśas.

He mentions four states of kleśas here: dormant, weak, interrupted, and
active. Dormant kleśas are 'roasted like burnt seeds' and cannot come back
again. The weak kleśas are going towards being dormant but can still come
back given the right stimulus. The last two states, interrupted and active, are
at full power but can swapped out for another one, for example, if you are
happy thinking of your significant other, and you are in a car accident, your
rāga/attraction will probably be swapped out for abhiniveśaḥ/fear-of-death.
But it can come back again after you survive and recover from the accident.
The fully/strongly active kleśa is the one currently in control. <u>The thing to
remember here is that you want to get rid of the kleśas by slowly making
them weaker until they are like 'roasted seeds'.</u>

II.5 अनित्याशुचि दुःखानात्मसु नित्य शुचि सुखात्म ख्यातिरविद्या

anitya aśuci duḥkha anātmasu nitya śuci sukha ātma khyātiḥ avidyā

"not eternal, not pure, painful, not self, eternal, pure, joyful, self, discrimination, ignorance"

Avidyā is ignorance. In II.2 Patañjali said that the kleśas are obstacles to samādhi, and in II.3 he listed the five kleśas, followed by the first definition of avidyā. Here he continues his definition of avidyā. It is further defined as the ignorance that the non-self (prakṛti), which is painful, unclean, and temporary, is different from the self (puruṣa), which is joyful, pure, and eternal. The non-self is anything in prakṛti, so you think that objects, such as the world, are eternal when they aren't, bodies are pure when they aren't, and painful things are pleasurable. <u>In other words, avidyā is the ignorance of the difference between puruṣa and prakṛti. This ignorance is what you need to get rid of to attain mokṣa. You get rid of it by acquiring discriminative wisdom (viveka khyātiḥ).</u> Patañjali discusses this in sūtras II.15 – II.28 and then gives his eight limbs of Aṣṭāṅga Yoga as the method to get this wisdom.

Remember from the first chapter that to get to mokṣa (the goal of yoga) you need to first get to samādhi. Therefore, since the kleśas are obstacles to samādhi, you need to get rid of them, so you can get the knowledge of the difference between puruṣa and prakṛti, which is what this kleśa is all about.

Note that he says that the puruṣa is eternal, pure, and joyful, so that when you attain mokṣa you are in a joyful state forever (see I.3).

II.6 दृग्दर्शन शक्त्योरेकात्मतेवास्मिता

dṛk darśana śaktyoḥ eka ātmatā iva asmitā

"consciousness force of the seer, of seeing, of the powers, one, self, as if, ego"

Asmitā is ego. This is when the mind considers the seer (puruṣa) to be the same as the mind (buddhi). Patañjali defines this as asmitā, which means 'I am-ness', or ego, i.e. there's a 'me'. Ego here is simply the notion of a 'me' and 'not me'. This one is very close to avidyā in that, in avidyā, you can't tell the difference between puruṣa and buddhi. With asmitā, your buddhi thinks that it's the same as the puruṣa.

I find his definition a bit obscure, but the important thing here is that Patañjali is defining the notion of 'I' as an additional kleśa. An acquaintance of mine, Śrīvatsa Ramaswami, once said that once there's a you, then there are things you like, things you dislike, and a fear of not being. Patañjali addresses these in the next three sūtras.

Vyāsa says that the consciousness force of the seer supplies the power of the sense of sight, and the buddhi has the power of being the instrument of seeing.

This kleśa works for the other powers of the senses: hearing, smelling, etc., but only one was needed to make his definition of 'I'.

II.7 सुखानुशयी रागः

sukha anuśayī rāgaḥ

"pleasure, after, attachment"

Rāga is attraction. This is defined as, based on a memory (which is the 'after'), the desire for something. Note that you have to have had an experience and therefore a memory to have an attraction to something. If you've never had an experience of something, you can't know whether you are attracted to it or not. In the Bhagavad Gītā, Kṛṣṇa says that a man of steady wisdom doesn't get happy when good/pleasant things are coming and doesn't get upset when bad things are coming. Rāga and the next kleśa, dveṣa, are a restatement and clarification of I.15 and I.16 where he defines vairāgya, or non-attachment. This doesn't mean that yogīs are dull and uninteresting people. Most people fluctuate from happiness to sadness, but yogīs just stay in a state of bliss that's beyond emotions.

II.8 दुःखानुशयी द्वेषः

duḥkha anuśayī dveṣaḥ
"pain, after, aversion"

Dveṣa is aversion. This is the same as rāga but it's an aversion to something based on a memory. I've seen this one defined as hate, but that's not quite right. If you have an experience you didn't like, you have an aversion to it, but you don't necessarily hate it. For example, if you eat something that you don't like, you don't hate it, but you dislike it. It's just that your buddhi has decided that it's something that you don't want, and can be as simple as disliking a certain food.

II.9 स्व रस वाही विदुषोऽपि तथा रूढोऽभिनिवेशः

sva rasa vāhī viduṣaḥ api tathā rūḍhaḥ abhiniveśaḥ
"own, desire, carrying, learned person, even, as well as, established, fear
   of death"

Abhiniveśaḥ is fear of death/clinging to life. It's really a fear of not 'being' anymore and is caused by not 'knowing' that you will continue after your body dies. Since none of us remember dying, or previous lives (at least most of us don't), we don't 'know' that we will be reborn/reincarnated. Interestingly, Patañjali says that abhiniveśaḥ affects even the wise, or advanced yogīs, so at least we're in good company here. Taimni says that if we truly 'know' that we are puruṣa and that we will continue after the body dies, why would we cling to life? I always liked that comment.

II.10 ते प्रतिप्रसव हेयाः सूक्ष्माः

te prati prasava heyāḥ sūkṣmāḥ
"those, going backwards, setting in motion, abandoned, subtle"

Here Patañjali says that the (kleśas) are subtle, and you get rid of them by reversing their evolution out of avidyā (ignorance). The commentators tend to say that the 'going backwards' is 'merging into their cause', which just means that they become dormant and can't come back again. Patañjali said that there are 4 states of the kleśas, from dormant to fully active (see II.4

above). As you move further along your path, you will slowly get rid of attraction and aversion as you realize that they are just about things and therefore unimportant. And sooner or later you will lose the fear of death, and, via samādhi, realize that you aren't really the body/mind, getting rid of asmitā (ego). At some point you realize the difference between you (puruṣa) and not-you (prakṛti, body/mind), thus getting rid of avidyā (ignorance). Once you've done this and get into asamprajñāta samādhi, you will disconnect from prakṛti, thus getting rid of your mind, and have attained the state of mokṣa.

Patañjali uses the word pratiprasava for this process of going backwards and abandoning the kleśas, because you can't actually destroy the kleśas, the best you can do is to make them dormant. There are differing opinions on what order you 'get rid' of the kleśas. One opinion is that you need to get rid of them in reverse order that Patañjali introduced them, and another is that you need to get rid of the last three in any order, followed by the first two in reverse order. Once they are dormant, they are like roasted seeds and can't become active again.

II.11 ध्यान हेयास्तद्वृत्तयः

dhyāna heyāḥ tad vrittayaḥ

"meditation, eliminated, those, vṛttis"

Here Patañjali says how to get rid of the kleśas: by meditation. He uses the word meditation here instead of samādhi, but I think samādhi would be more precise since you use meditation (dhyāna) to get samādhi, and samādhi is his solution to attain mokṣa, which is what his entire treatise is about. Note that the first chapter is called "Samādhi Pāda". Everything else is just to support that main idea.

He uses the word vṛttis here to indicate that the kleśas cause mental fluctuations, and as he said in the first chapter, you need to stop them.

Section Summary

In this section Patañjali gives what the beginning yogī needs to work on, i.e. Kriyā Yoga, which includes tapas (austerity), svādhyāya (study), and Īśvara praṇidhāna (surrender to Īśvara). He then introduces the five kleśas (obstacles/obstructions): avidyā, asmitā, rāga, dveṣa, and abhiniveṣāḥ. He finally says that you get rid of them by meditation.

II.12 – II.14 Karma

In II.1 – II.11 Patañjali discusses Kriyā Yoga and the kleśas (obstructions) to attaining mokṣa. The kleśas cause you to act, whether to get something you're attracted to, to stay away from something you are averse to, or to stay alive. In the next three sūtras, he discusses how these actions affect you in this life and future lives. Remember that reincarnation is fundamental to Hindu philosophy.

Let's start with the definition of karma: action (mental or physical). The result of the action is its fruit. So when something bad happens to someone, and other people say "that's bad karma," indicating the 'something bad' is the bad karma, this is not really correct. The 'something bad' is actually the fruit of a previous adharmic/non-virtuous action. The same applies to 'something good.' It's the fruit of a previous dharmic/virtuous action.

In Hinduism there is the concept of dharma, which is your duty in this lifetime, i.e. righteous action. It encompasses what your station in life, your caste if you are in ancient India, and specifies what you should do or not do. Adharma is anything that is contrary to your dharma, i.e. unrighteous action. Two words that are also used instead of dharma/adharma are punya/apunya, and these mean, respectively, virtuous and non-virtuous.

Sometimes apunya and adharma are translated as 'sin.' But this is a misleading translation, especially in the West, where in some religions enough 'sin' will get you eternal suffering in 'hell.' Hinduism doesn't have the concept of eternal suffering for bad actions, but you do go to hell for awhile to pay for your bad actions, and then you get born again. The same is true for good actions getting you to heaven (the celestial realms) and then getting reborn again. How you get out of this cycle of rebirth is discussed by Patañjali in II.15 – II.28.

So the concept of karma is that good/dharmic/punya actions have good results/fruit, and bad/adharmic/apunya actions have bad results/fruit. I have heard someone say that karma means bad actions and dharma applies to good actions, but this isn't true. Karma applies to both good and bad actions.

In II.1 – II.11 Patañjali discussed the concept of kleśas and the five types of kleśas. The kleśas cause vṛttis which cause actions/karma which cause saṃskāras, which sets us up for tending to respond the in the same way to later instances of the same experience. So now that we know about kleśas, Patañjali is going to talk about how actions affect you and your path/journey (sādhana).

II.12 क्लेश मूलः कर्माशयो दृष्टादृष्ट जन्म वेदनीयः

kleśa mūlaḥ karma āśayaḥ dṛṣṭa adṛṣṭa janma vedanīyaḥ

"obstructions, root, action, repository, seen, unseen, births, to be experienced"

The karmāśaya is a new term that means the repository of karma; the word āśaya means a repository/receptacle. I like to think of the karmāśaya as a knapsack that you keep with you from life to life. I haven't seen anything that describes how this works, but in Indian philosophy it's assumed that the karmāśaya is somehow attached to the puruṣa in between lives. If it wasn't then one person could get the results of someone else's karma which would invalidate the entire idea of karma. It's fairly obvious that the karmāśaya, while it exists, is subtle, another basic Indic philosophy concept. So, since the puruṣa is also subtle, and without a better explanation, I'm going to assume that there's subtle super glue that sticks them together. There are different ideas on where the karmāśaya exists, but Patañjali doesn't discuss it since it's not important for his text. The important thing to know is that the record of all your karma is stored in the karmāśaya and follows you from life to life.

In this sūtra, Patañjali says that the karmāśaya has its root in the kleśas, which cause karma, and the fruits of those actions are experienced either in the seen/current or unseen/future life.

II.13 सति मूले तद्विपाको जात्यायुर्भोगाः

sati mūle tad vipākaḥ jāti āyuḥ bhogāḥ

"being present, root, that, fruits in, species, life-span, experience"

In II.12 Patañjali discussed that actions in this life will cause fruit later in this life, or in a future life. Here he defines how karma affects your future lives. He says that as long as you have kleśas you will do karma and those actions determine the species (human, dog, tree, etc.) that you will be born in, the length of that life, and how much pain and pleasure you'll have in that life.

II.14 ते ह्लाद परिताप फलाः पुण्यापुण्य हेतुत्वात्

te hlāda paritāpa phalāḥ puṇya apuṇya hetutvāt

"these, pleasure, pain, fruit, virtuous, non-virtuous, caused by"

In this sūtra Patañjali finishes his discussion of karma by saying that the pleasant and unpleasant results/fruits have their cause in good or bad actions. So good actions result in pleasurable fruit and bad actions result in unpleasant fruit.

Section Summary

In this section, Patañjali says that as long as you haven't managed to get rid of the kleśas you will continue to do karma (action), and those actions will affect your future lives, in the species, length of life, and how much pain and pleasure you'll have. He also says that the karmas that you haven't yet experienced the fruit of is carried in the karmāśaya from life to life. He finishes up saying that virtuous actions get good results, while non-virtuous actions get bad results.

II.15 – II.28 Cause and Goal of Yoga Sādhana

Pain/suffering is real and can/should be avoided. This is part of at least three philosophies – Sāṃkhya, Patañjali, and Buddhism. Sāṃkhya says that there are three types of pain: internal, external, and unforeseen external causes (in fact this is the very first sūtra in the Sāṃkhya Kārikā). Patañjali says the same thing, except he says everything is painful, with slightly different reasons: you don't have something you want, or you have something you are afraid of losing, and everything always changes. The four noble truths of Buddhism are suffering is real, there is a cause for suffering, suffering can be ended, and there is a path that removes the suffering.

<u>Why should we take up the yogic path? Because the goal of yoga is moksa, or liberation from suffering.</u> Patañjali provides a set of practices to get rid of suffering in the second chapter in sūtras 29 – 55 and the first three sūtras of the third chapter. Before he does this, however, he gives us a discussion of suffering (i.e. why we want to take up yoga), says that it can be ended, how this fits into the dichotomy of puruṣa and prakṛti from the first chapter, and some high level discussion on removing the suffering.

In I.2 योगश्चित्त वृत्ति निरोधः "yogaś citta vṛtti nirodhaḥ" (yoga is the stilling of the fluctuations of the mind), Patañjali states that yoga is samādhi (see Vyāsa's commentary on I.1 as mentioned in I.2). Once you are in the state of yoga, then I.3 तदा द्रष्टुः स्वरूपेऽवस्थानम् "tadā draṣṭuḥ svarūpe 'vasthānam" (then the seer abides in its own form) comes into play, answering the question of "then what?" in response to I.2. The drashta is the puruṣa/self. Abiding in it's true form means being in the state of kaivalyam, or absolute aloneness. This happens when you get into asamprajñāta samādhi (I.51).

Now we know the goal, but the question is why we should care about attaining mokṣa and why would we want to start on the yogic path, or sādhana. Patañjali, and also Sāṃkhya both say the same thing: suffering.

Sāṃkhya 1 and 2 (paraphrased): when you are afflicted by the three kinds of suffering: internal, external/due-to-nature, and unforeseen external causes, you want to know how to get rid of the suffering. This is not superfluous because, while ordinary remedies exist, they aren't permanent or complete. Remedies from scripture are like ordinary ones in that they are subject to impurity, decay, and various levels of effectiveness. A better remedy is the knowledge of prakṛti (matter and the mind), both unmanifest and manifest, and of the puruṣa (the true self).

In II.15 Patañjali says that to the one with discrimination everything is suffering. In II.17 he says that the conjunction of prakṛti and puruṣa, i.e. having a body, is the cause of the suffering. In II.24 he says that the cause of the conjunction is avidyā (ignorance) of the difference between prakṛti and puruṣa. In II.25 he says that with the removal of the ignorance, the conjunction is removed. This is the absolute freedom of the seer (Bryant's translation II.25). In II.28 he says that you get rid of the impurities and gain knowledge, culminating in discriminative wisdom (viveka khyātiḥ) by following the eight limbs of Aṣṭāṅga Yoga. I personally think that II.15-II.28 are the most important in the sutras because they give what we are trying to do and why.

II.15 परिणाम ताप संस्कार दुःखैर्गुण वृत्ति विरोधाच्च दुःखमेव सर्वं विवेकिनः

pariṇāma tāpa saṃskāra du:khaiḥ guṇa vṛtti virodhāt ca du:kham eva
    sarvaṃ vivekinaḥ
"result, pain, mental impression, due to pain, guṇa, fluctuation, obstruc-
    tion, and, pain, only, everything, one that has discrimination"

<u>Here Patañjali tells us why we should want to start yoga; because of suffering.</u> He says that, to the one with discrimination, everything is suffering, due to experience (which causes saṃskāras – mental impressions), and the ever-changing guṇas; not having something that you want is suffering, having something and worrying about losing it is suffering, and also knowing that everything is always changing and not knowing what is coming next is suffering. But the good news is that, both according to Sāṃkhya and Patañjali, you can permanently get rid of suffering. Patañjali spends sutras II.15 – II.28 discussing this.

He brings back the term, 'guṇas' here. To remind you, the guṇas are qualities, not a thing that you can touch. All prakṛti, from gross matter up to primordial prakṛti (pradhāna) has these three qualities, which are sattva (light, peaceful, quiet), rajas (heat, activity), and tamas (inactivity, inertia, darkness). The point is that everything in matter can be described using various amounts or ratios of these three guṇas.

It may seem like it's the puruṣa that realizes that everything is pain, but that's not true. Many of the commentators are not clear about this. Remember that the philosophy is that the puruṣa doesn't, and in fact, cannot change. Realizing something is a change, i.e. it didn't know something before, and now it does. So it's the buddhi that realizes that everything is pain. Once it realizes that, it then needs to figure out how to get rid of the pain, and according to Patañjali and the other mokṣa traditions, the way to do that is to not be reborn. This is because pain, of any sort, can only be in prakṛti: puruṣa can't feel pain but it can see that the buddhi is in pain (mental and physical). <u>To be very clear here, it's the buddhi that has the desire to follow the yogic path, not the puruṣa.</u> There's more on this in my commentary on II.23.

The idea that everything is suffering can be objected to by noting that life can be very enjoyable, so why would anyone want to discard the pleasures of life? An answer can be found in 2.8 of the Taittirīya Upaniṣad, where it says that the bliss of a person that is young, strong, solidly built, and also owns the whole world with all its wealth, is one measure of bliss. Then it goes on to list ten levels of celestial beings, all the way up to the divine, and it states that, at each level, one measure of bliss at that level is the same as one hundred measures of bliss at the previous level. This comes out to ten trillion times the bliss of the original person is a single measure of bliss at the highest level!

II.16 हेयं दुःखमनागतम्

heyaṃ du:kham anāgatam

"To be avoided, suffering, that hasn't yet occurred"

So after saying that everything is suffering, he now says that you can, and should avoid, future suffering. This is a very hopeful intro to the rest of this section.

II.17 द्रष्टृ दृष्ययोः संयोगो हेय हेतुः

drastr drsyayoḥ samyogaḥ heya hetuḥ
"seer, seen, conjunction, to be avoided, cause"

Patañjali says that the cause of the suffering to be avoided is the conjunction of the puruṣa and prakṛti, i.e. being born. Because of the conjunction (samyoga) you keep getting reborn, which is probably why he discussed karma just before this topic, since it deals with and affects your current and future lives. In the mokṣa philosophies, rebirth is a tragedy because it means that you haven't attained mokṣa yet.

Here he uses two new terms for the puruṣa (seer/draṣtṛ) and prakṛti (seen/dṛṣya), probably to keep the text interesting. Since the puruṣa is unmanifest, and the buddhi, ahaṃkāra, etc. are manifest, they can't actually touch, so conjunction is a good word for this association.

II.18 प्रकाश क्रिया स्थिति शिलं भूतेन्द्रियात्मकं भोगापवर्गार्थं दृश्यम्

prakāśa kriyā sthiti śilaṃ bhūta indriya ātmakaṃ bhoga apavarga arthaṃ
    dṛśyam
"illumination, activity, inertia, of the character, elements, senses, con-
    sisting of, experience, liberation, purpose, of the seen"

Here Patañjali uses the new words, prakāśa (illumination/sattva), kriyā (activity/rajas), sthiti (inertia/tamas), and apavarga (liberation/mokṣa).

In the previous sūtra he brought up the idea that the cause of suffering is the conjunction of puruṣa and prakṛti. So now he's going to talk about prakṛti. He says that it has the guṇas (sattva, rajas, tamas) as its qualities, and also says that the purpose of prakṛti is for experience or liberation. If you are not interested in attaining mokṣa then prakṛti just provides experiences through the senses. If you are interested in attaining mokṣa, then prakṛti is used by you to provide experiences, through yoga, to get the knowledge of the difference between puruṣa and prakṛti that brings you to liberation.

The obstacles to this knowledge are the kleśas, II.1 – II.11. The kleśa of asmitā (ego) makes you think that your body and mind are your true self, whereas your true self is actually your puruṣa. The kleśa of avidyā (ignorance) is related to asmitā, in that, with avidyā, you think that your body and mind are permanent, pure, and painless, instead of actually being impermanent, impure, and full of pain.

There is some confusion/disagreement as to the word 'guṇa'. Pretty much all Indic philosophies agree that prakṛti exists (in Advaita Vedanta, only if you look at it the right way), and that prakṛti has three guṇas: sattva, rajas, and tamas. The problem is whether the guṇas are 'things' or 'qualities'. Some people use the guṇas as something that you could possibly see or touch. This is wrong because the guṇas are qualities that can be used to describe many things, prakṛti being one of them. They can also be used to describe people; highly advanced yogīs are sattvic, people trying to get ahead in business are very rājasic, and criminals are tāmasic (because they are dark, ignorant, etc.). While people are made up of prakṛti, you would use different guṇas to describe the same person depending on how they feel. For example if a person normally has a bright, sunny disposition, you would call them sattvic. If, however, one day they are depressed, you would say that they are tāmasic at that time.

II.19 विशेषाविशेष लिङ्गमात्रालिङ्गानि गुण पर्वाणि

viśeṣa aviśeṣa liṅgamātra aliṅgāni guṇa parvāṇi

"specific, non-specific, effect/product, undefined, guṇas, the states of"

Patañjali is continuing his discussion of prakṛti in this sūtra. He says that the guṇas have four states/levels: specific (gross matter, the powers of the knowledge and action senses, and manas), non-specific (subtle matter and ahaṃkāra), 'effect/product' (buddhi), and undefined (primordial prakṛti/ pradhāna). Different translators use different words than the ones I've used, but they're all good. I used effect/product because buddhi devolves from pradhāna, a product, and it is the cause, an effect, of the ahaṃkāra.

These four states correlate to the devolutes (levels or entities) in the Sāṃkhya tree I keep talking about. If you remember, gross matter is space/ether/ākāśa, wind/vāyu, fire/tejas, water/ap, and earth/pṛthvī. Subtle matter is sound/śabda, touch/sparśa, form/rūpa, taste/rasa, smell/gandha. Primordial prakṛti (pradhāna) is prakṛti before it's 'touched' by puruṣa: all the guṇas are in equal proportions in pradhāna, and it's all homogeneous. I like to compare it to oatmeal: you can't tell that there are parts because it's all the same everywhere.

The word liṅgamātra can be translated a number of ways: it's generally translated as 'indicator only', but I prefer 'the effect or product (that which is evolved out of a primary cause and itself becomes a producer).' Since buddhi (the intellect) is 'devolved' out of the primary cause, primordial prakṛti (pradhāna), and ahaṃkāra is 'devolved' out of it, this makes sense. See Appendix F for more on this.

The word 'undefined' for primordial prakṛti is because, first, it's all the same as I've noted above, but also because it's not manifest and can't be 'seen' by the buddhi, or any of the other devolutes for that matter, since it's more subtle than all the devolutes and Sāṃkhya says that something can't directly perceive anything that is more subtle than 'itself.' Since it can't be perceived it's undefined.

II.20 द्रष्टा दृशि मात्रः शुद्धोऽपि प्रत्ययानुपश्यः

> drāṣṭā dṛśi mātraḥ śuddhaḥ api pratyaya anupaśyaḥ
>
> "seer, seeing, only, pure, although, contents of the mind, sees "

The puruṣa (seer) is pure consciousness, but it 'sees' the contents of the mind (pratyaya). Since the puruṣa doesn't have a body, and therefore eyes, it doesn't actually 'see', but it is conscious of the contents of the buddhi.

After having discussed prakṛti, Patañjali now discusses the puruṣa so we know how it fits in with his statement that everything being painful and how to get rid of the pain. 'Seeing only' means that puruṣa is unchangeable: the only thing puruṣa can do is to 'see', nothing else, and therefore is 'seeing only'. This is important because puruṣa and prakṛti have different purposes and capabilities, and we need to understand them both so that we can understand the following sūtras.

II.21 तदर्थ एव दृश्यस्यात्मा

tad arthaḥ eva dṛśyasya ātmā

"that, purpose, only, of the seen, puruṣa"

Patañjali continues on his discussion of puruṣa and prakṛti, saying that the only purpose of prakṛti (the seen) is enabling puruṣa to attain mokṣa (see II.18). Of course it also gives experience for people that aren't interested in attaining mokṣa but we don't care about that here.

II.22 कृतार्थं प्रति नष्टमप्यनष्टं तदन्य साधारणत्वात्

kṛta arthaṃ prati naṣṭam api anaṣṭam tad anya sādhāraṇatvāt

"accomplished, purpose, with regard to, ceases to exist, although, still
     exists, that, other, because of being common"

Here Patañjali discusses what happens to prakṛti when a yogī gets rid of the conjunction (II.17) of puruṣa, and prakṛti, and attains mokṣa (which is the purpose/goal of yoga). He says that once the puruṣa attains mokṣa, prakṛti 'ceases to exist' for that puruṣa, but since prakṛti is common to all puruṣas, it still exists for them. By 'ceases to exist' he's referring to I.3 and I.51 where he said that in mokṣa the puruṣa has completely disconnected from prakṛti. But while it doesn't exist for that puruṣa, it still does for all the other puruṣas that haven't yet attained mokṣa. Remember that every puruṣa is connected to prakṛti until prakṛti disconnects itself from puruṣa. This is also in line with this philosophy's idea that puruṣa and prakṛti always exist.

II.23. स्व स्वामि शत्त्योः स्व रुपोपलब्धि हेतुः संयोगः

sva svāmi śaktyoḥ sva rupa upalabdhi hetuḥ saṃyogaḥ
"possessed, possessor, of the powers, own, nature, realization, caused,
  conjunction"

Here, Patañjali says that the conjunction is the means of understanding
the true nature and powers of both prakṛti (possessed) and puruṣa
(possessor). Patañjali is again using some different words for puruṣa and
prakṛti. The idea here is that using the body/mind together, the buddhi can
determine and understand both itself and puruṣa. Remember that you attain
mokṣa by truly understanding the difference between puruṣa and prakṛti, as
I've discussed before.

I'm going to get into a deeper philosophical discussion for the rest of
my commentary on this sūtra. You can skip this if you like.

One question that I had for a long time here is which entity, puruṣa or
prakṛti, determines to follow the yogic path and which one understands the
difference mentioned above. The answer is not obvious without more information. Remember that the puruṣa is immutable, so it can't change (see II.20,
IV.18, and Sāṃkhya 18). It is simply pure consciousness. Prakṛti, which here
is the body/mind complex is changeable and makes decisions.

Sāṃkhya says in 18 that the puruṣa is immutable and is not an agent, i.e.
it can't/doesn't do anything, including telling the buddhi what to do. This is
one of the main assumptions in both Sāṃkhya and Patañjali (II.20, IV.18):
that the puruṣa is immutable, or cannot change. If it can't change, it can't
realize or think about anything: it's just consciousness. It also can't do
anything such as telling or controlling the buddhi to follow the yogic path to
attain mokṣa. Since it is immutable it also cannot be bound or liberated. Even
if it could it wouldn't care since it can't change or be changed, i.e. be
impacted by being bound.

Since puruṣa can't change, it can't get new knowledge about anything,
in particular about puruṣa and prakṛti. But it's also conscious of what is going
on in the buddhi, and the buddhi changes. The knowledge of these changes
would require a change to puruṣa if it isn't omniscient. So it has to be
omniscient. We also know that it's omniscient because in I.24 Patañjali said
that Īśvara is a special puruṣa, but still a puruṣa. Then in I.25 he said that
Īśvara's omniscience is unsurpassed (see I.25 for some thoughts on

omniscience), which implies that other things are 'omniscient'. The only other things that could be omniscient are puruṣa and prakṛti. I've already shown that puruṣa is omniscient (since it's the same as Īśvara except it's not special). Interestingly enough, in IV.31, Patañjali says that the buddhi also becomes essentially omniscient.

Because of this, it's up to the buddhi to figure it out and get the knowledge. Once it's got that knowledge, it unbinds or disconnects itself from puruṣa, thus attaining mokṣa. So the buddhi determines that everything is painful/non-satisfying, determines the difference between puruṣa and prakṛti, and disconnects from puruṣa (see Sāṃkhya 63). Note that since it's not attached to the puruṣa anymore, and subtle matter is what makes up a person (buddhi, ahaṃkāra, manas, the powers of the senses), those things just go back into primordial prakṛti (pradhāna).

Some people think that the puruṣa 'learns' from the experience mentioned in II.18. The problem with this is that, according to Patañjali, the puruṣa is immutable; if the puruṣa realizes something, that's a change. The only thing that can change in Patañjali's philosophy is prakṛti, and it's always changing. Therefore the only thing that is realizing anything is the buddhi.

In summary, it's up to the buddhi to figure it out, using the eight limbs of Aṣṭāṅga Yoga described in the second half of the second chapter. The buddhi determines that it's in pain and follows the yogic path to get rid of that pain. It uses the first seven limbs of Aṣṭāṅga to get to samādhi where it will figure out the difference between puruṣa and prakṛti. When it figures this out it knows that it's not the real self (puruṣa) and needs to be 'destroyed' in order to stop the pain.

Sūtras II.24 – II.28 continue the discussion of how discriminative knowledge (viveka khyātiḥ) allows you to attain mokṣa, and how to do it.

II.24 तस्य हेतुरविद्या

tasya hetuḥ avidyā
"its, cause, ignorance"

This sūtra is very simple and straightforward. He says that the cause of the conjunction of puruṣa and prakṛti (saṃyoga) is avidyā/ignorance. Here he's tying it back to the discussion on kleśas at the beginning of the chapter. So the cause of the conjunction and therefore pain is due to the kleśas, and you have kleśas because you were born, and you were born because you have avidyā. Vyāsa says in his commentary that when the knowledge of the puruṣa is acquired, and therefore knowledge of prakṛti, the function of buddhi ends. He goes on to say that because then it's unbound, it does not appear again.

II.25 तदभावात् संयोगाभावो हानं तद् दृशोः कैवल्यम्

tad abhāvāt saṃyoga abhāvaḥ hānaṃ tad dṛśeḥ kaivalyam
"that, due to absence, conjunction, disappears, end, that, seer,
    liberation/absolute aloneness"

The Saṃskṛtam here is a bit obscure, but to translate it into English, it says that due to the absence of ignorance the conjunction of puruṣa and prakṛti ends/disappears, and that ending is the liberation of the seer (puruṣa). Vyāsa says that when the avidyā/ignorance ends the conjunction, bondage and pain are ended permanently: this is kaivalyam/mokṣa. He also reiterates that there is no further contact between the puruṣa and prakṛti. Finally, he says that in that state the puruṣa remains established in itself (see I.3). This sūtra shows that yoga is about separation, not union: the goal is to separate puruṣa and prakṛti. There's no union in Patañjali's definition of mokṣa.

Mokṣa is the concept of liberation; kaivalyam is Patañjali's specific definition of mokṣa (see Appendix D for a discussion of some alternative views on mokṣa). The definition of kaivalyam is detachment of the puruṣa from matter/perfect isolation/final emancipation.

What is mokṣa like? Patañjali says that it's the perfect isolation of the puruṣa (kaivalyam). In his definition of avidyā (II.5), he said that the puruṣa is eternal, pure, and joyful. So the puruṣa, which by definition can't change, always has those three qualities, including when in mokṣa. Patañjali said in II.15 that to the one with discrimination, everything is painful. From my commentary up to now it should be obvious that the pain is only felt in the body/mind. Therefore, to get rid of the pain we need to get rid of our prakṛtic self. To do that we have to not get reborn, i.e. attain mokṣa. So, in mokṣa, you have no pain because you don't have a body anymore, and your puruṣa is in an eternal, pure, and joyful state.

To tie this into the first chapter, kaivalyam/mokṣa occurs in asamprajñāta samādhi where your puruṣa is disconnected from prakṛti and can only be conscious of itself, i.e. in a state of kaivalyam. Patañjali, in I.51, said that asamprajñāta (he uses the word nirbīja) samādhi leads to attaining mokṣa.

The question may be asked "who actually desires to end life and become 'body free'"? The fundamental desire in the mokṣa traditions is to experience a situation/state after death that is much better than what you can experience in life. To be 'body free' is exactly what Patañjali says a yogī wants: to get rid of all the suffering (II.15-II.28). In II.5, Patañjali defines avidyā (ignorance), as being ignorant of the self (puruṣa) with the not-self (prakṛti). Once you get rid of the avidyā, you realize that the prakṛtic self is not you, that suffering is only in the prakṛtic self, and therefore you want to get rid of it. <u>Getting rid of your prakṛtic self gives you kaivalyam, Patañjali's definition of liberation/mokṣa.</u>

The Chandogya Upaniṣad (another ancient text) shows that Patañjali isn't the only philosophy that wants to be 'body free'. 8.12.1 of the Chandogya Upaniṣad says that if you have a body, you have pain and pleasure, and there's no freedom from pain and pleasure if you have a body. It continues, saying that pain and pleasure don't affect you if you don't have a body. This shows that, as I mentioned before, that in many Indian philosophies, to attain mokṣa you can't have a body, i.e. you're dead.

II.26. विवेक ख्यातिरविप्लवा हानोपायः

viveka khyātiḥ aviplavā hāna upāyaḥ

"discriminative, wisdom, uninterrupted, cessation, method"

Patañjali adds a bit more to the previous sūtra here. In the previous one he said that getting rid of avidyā/ignorance is how to attain mokṣa. Here he says that once you have gotten rid of avidyā, you need uninterrupted viveka khyātiḥ (discriminative wisdom) to actually attain mokṣa. Vyāsa says that discriminative wisdom is the knowledge of the difference between puruṣa and prakṛti. When the avidyā reaches the state of a burnt seed (and can't come back again), that uninterrupted knowledge is the means of attaining liberation/mokṣa.

II.27 तस्य सप्तधा प्रान्त भूमिः प्रज्ञा

tasya saptadhā prānta bhūmiḥ prajñā

"his, sevenfold, final, ground, prajna"

Here Patañjali says that in the final stage of the practice of yoga, there is a sevenfold wisdom. Patañjali doesn't specify what these levels are but Vyāsa does.

1. The knowledge of pain is complete. There's nothing left to know.
2. The knowledge of the cause of pain, the kleśas, is complete, and the kleśas are in the state of 'roasted seeds'.
3. Knowledge that the conjunction of puruṣa and prakṛti will be removed is complete, due to realization from samādhi.
4. The knowledge from uninterrupted discriminative wisdom, the means of attaining mokṣa is complete.
5. The knowledge that the buddhi's intelligence and sentience have done their job and are no longer needed is complete.
6. The knowledge that the prakṛtic body will disconnect from puruṣa is complete.
7. The knowledge that the puruṣa will attain mokṣa once prakṛti has separated from it is complete.

II.28 योगाङ्गानुष्ठानादशुद्धि क्षये ज्ञान दीप्तिराविवेक ख्यातेः

yoga aṅga anusthānāt aśuddhi kṣaye jñāna dīptiḥ ā viveka khyāteḥ

"yoga, limbs, through practice, impurities, upon elimination, knowledge, light, up to, discriminative, wisdom"

This is the final sūtra in this section. Patañjali says that by the practice
of the limbs of yoga, the impurities (kleśas) are eliminated, giving knowledge
and light, and leading up to discriminative wisdom (viveka khyātiḥ). So you
get the discriminative wisdom that ends in mokṣa by practicing the limbs of
yoga. This sūtra is also a segue into the rest of the chapter on the first five of
the eight limbs of Aṣṭāṅga Yoga, where he gives the various requirements
and practices needed to get the discriminative wisdom.

Section Summary

In this section, Patañjali gives the reasons for following the yogic path –
to avoid pain, and the fact that future pain can be avoided. He discusses how
puruṣa and prakṛti fit into the yogic path, and finishes up discussing how the
pain is caused by avidyā (ignorance), which is caused by being born. He also
notes that once you get rid of avidyā (ignorance) you won't get born again,
which is mokṣa/kaivalyam. He finishes up by saying that you get the
knowledge to remove ignorance by following the limbs of Aṣṭāṅga Yoga.

II.29 – II.45 The Eight Limbs, Yamas, Niyamas

So far in the second chapter Patañjali has discussed Kriyā Yoga, (consisting of tapas (effort/austerity), svādhyāya (study), and Īśvara praṇidhāna (surrender to Īśvara)), the kleśas (obstructions), karma (action), the reason to follow the yogic path, i.e pain, and a high-level description of how to attain mokṣa. For the rest of this chapter he discusses the first five of the eight limbs of Aṣṭāṅga Yoga (please note that this is different than Aṣṭāṅga Vinyasa Yoga, the āsana practice taught by Pattabhi Jois). Patañjali discusses the external limbs (the first five) in this chapter and the internal limbs (the last three) in the next chapter. In this section I'm going to discuss the first two limbs and the results from perfecting them.

II.29 यम नियमासन प्राणायाम प्रत्याहार धारणा ध्यान

समाधयोऽष्टावङ्गानि

yama niyama āsana prāṇāyāma pratyāhāra dhāraṇā dhyāna samādhayaḥ
    aṣṭau aṅgāni
"ethics/restraints, observances/attitudes, posture, increasing prāṇa, sense
    withdrawal, concentration, meditation, samādhi, eight, limbs"

Patañjali said in II.28 that by practicing the limbs of yoga, you get the discriminative wisdom (viveka khyātiḥ) that you need to attain mokṣa. In this sūtra he just lists all eight of the limbs. The following sūtras discuss each one in detail. The limbs are

1. yama – ethical restraints
2. niyama – observances and attitudes
3. āsana – postures
4. prāṇāyāma – increasing/expanding prāṇa in the body
5. pratyāhāra – withdrawing from the senses
6. dhāraṇā – concentration
7. dhyāna – meditation
8. samādhi – tool for getting discriminative wisdom (viveka khyātiḥ)
    while in meditation

An acquaintance of mine, Śrīvatsa Ramaswami, once told me that these limbs are to get rid of distractions so you can get discriminative wisdom (viveka khyātiḥ). With the yamas, if you're not harming, lying, or stealing from people, then they won't be chasing you, beating you up, and throwing you in jail. The niyamas are observances and attitudes that remove other distractions, e.g., if you meditate in a clean place you won't have the distractions of a messy place reminding you of things that need to be done; if you are content with what you have you won't be distracted by the size of other's houses, cars, and vacations. Āsana gives you a strong, flexible, and healthy body so you can be comfortable when meditating. Prāṇāyāma, along with increasing prāṇa in the body, also balances the sleepy effects of the ida nadī with the monkey-mind effects of the piṅgala nadī, thus giving you a better meditation. Pratyāhāra disconnects the mind from sensory input so sensory distractions disappear during meditation.

The last three limbs are levels of meditation and will be discussed later.

II.30 अहिंसा सत्यास्तेय ब्रह्मचर्यापरिग्रहा यमाः

ahiṃsā satya asteya brahmacarya aparigrahāḥ yamāḥ

"Non-harming, non-lying, non-stealing, chastity, non-acceptance, yamas"

In this sūtra he lists all of the yamas:
- ahiṃsā – non harming
- satya – non lying
- asteya – non stealing
- brahmacarya – not having sex
- aparigraha – non acceptance of more than necessary

The yamas are a list of five ethical restraints, and the niyamas (II.32) are five observances and attitudes you should do and have. Some people look at them as a club to keep you in line with yogic practice, and that you're not a good yogī if you aren't following all of them perfectly, but to me that's hurtful and not helpful. Remember that yoga is a many lifetime practice and is a lot of hard work. I prefer to look at them as signposts that you are still making progress; if you honestly review yourself and find that you are getting better at doing them, or doing ones you didn't do before (maybe not perfectly), then you are making progress. Yoga is a practice that allows you to let go of the things that don't serve you anymore, so as you move along on your practice, you will be more in line with the yamas and niyamas, because you will naturally do them because you will find not doing them to be antithetical to yourself and your beliefs.

Ahimsā means not harming, but it's not possible to not harm anything while living. Harming includes thinking harm as well as physically doing harm (see II.34). Just driving your car kills bugs flying in the air, walking down the sidewalk will possibly kill ants and other bugs on the sidewalk, plowing a field will kill creatures living in the dirt. Hariharānanda says that ahimsā is something to work towards, and the ultimate expression of ahimsā is not to be born again, in which case you can't harm anything at all.

Satya and asteya (non-lying and non stealing) are fairly obvious.

Brahmacarya is problematic for some people. The definition of the word is celibacy, like it or not. Every commentator and dictionary that I checked agree with this. There are people that want to follow the yogic path and are unhappy with the idea of celibacy. They want to be yogīs but still want to have sex. Vyāsa says "Celibacy is the control of the secret organ." Bhārati says that just looking at, talking to, or touching a person of the opposite sex with desire is not practicing brahmacarya. So, brahmacarya is refraining from having any desire for anything doing with sex, whether that's thinking or acting.

The problem, from a yogic perspective, is that sex keeps you in and attached to prakṛti, and the goal is to completely separate from prakṛti.

Brahmacarya is a compound word that means celibacy. Some people, in order to get around the problem of celibacy try to change the definition of the word brahmacarya by breaking it up into two words, "brahma" and "carya," which then, according to them, means "walking with Brahman (the divine)", and therefore has nothing do with celibacy. This is pure sophistry though and does not accurately translate what Patañjali means here. Bhārati, in his commentary on II.38, says "It is not for nothing that celibacy is called 'walking with God' (brahma-carya)."

What does brahmacarya mean to people who desire to be on the yogic path but still want to have sex? To answer this I will start with the four stages of life in India. The first is called brahmacarya (celibacy), and is from birth to marriage. The second, gṛhastha (householder), is after getting married: sex is expected in this stage. In the third stage, vānaprastha (retired), the children have moved out and you focus on your spiritual practices: you are still married and sex is still ok. The fourth stage, saṃnyāsa (renunciation), you get rid of all your worldly possessions, leave your spouse, and become a wandering mendicant: there's no sex in this stage.

Given the above, how does brahmacarya fit into the yogic path? If you are born as an advanced yogī, you will not be interested in relationships, sex, or any related distractions, and you are going to be outside the four stages of life. If you are interested in relationships and sex, while you may be on the path, you are not an advanced yogī yet.

Aparigraha means non-acceptance of more than necessary. Aparigraha is sometimes translated as not being greedy, but this isn't really correct because that has the connotation of hoarding. Having things, especially pleasant things, causes saṃskāras due to the desire to keep those things and is therefore a distraction from your practice. Hariharānanda says that only things necessary for maintaining the body should be accepted. He also says that to preserve wealth without using it for the good of others is not aparigraha.

<u>Many people think that they have to immediately conform to all parts of the yogic path. This is ridiculous.</u> You can still work on your sādhana while being a gṛhastha (householder). Patañjali is giving the full list of things that you must do to be a yogī. Most, if not all of us, can't always maintain all the yamas and niyamas. Remember that yoga is a many-lifetime process and we are all working on our own sādhana. At some point you will be born as an advanced yogī and you will find that the yamas and niyamas are not a problem anymore.

II.31 जाति देश काल समयानवच्छिन्नाः सार्व भौमा महा व्रतम्

jāti deśa kāla samaya anavacchinnāḥ sārva bhaumāḥ mahā vratam
"species, place, time, situation, unconditional, all, on the earth, great,
   vow"

Here Patañjali says that a yogī has to always keep all the yamas, no matter what. As I mentioned before, this isn't always possible. However, in the sūtra style of writing, things in a list are in order of importance with the first being the most important and the last being the least important. So if you can't keep all the yamas, keep in mind which ones are the most important.

But you can be creative in your efforts to keep all of them. An interesting example is a story about a man that was being chased by criminals. He came to an āśrama and told the guru that he needed a place to hide. The guru told him where to hide. When the criminals came to the āśrama they told the guru that he needed to tell them where the man went. The guru responded that the mouth cannot speak of what the eyes have not seen. At this, the criminals left to look elsewhere. In this case the guru didn't violate the yama of satya (telling the truth), or the yama of ahimsā (non harming).

Patañjali doesn't say that this is just a vow (vrata), but a great vow (mahā vrata), and he says that it always applies: class, place, time, or circumstances are not excuses for breaking this vow. Vyāsa says that a fisherman that only kills fish but doesn't harm anything else, is an example of harming based on species, and is not allowed. Kshatriyas (warriors and rulers) are allowed by the culture to kill animals for food, and also during battle. However, this is not allowed by Patañjali. Vyāsa also says that only harming animals for religious purposes, on certain days and only in certain places (temples) is not allowed. So it's not possible to be a yogī and be a fisherman or kṣatriya, etc. Yogīs must hold to the yamas at all times, or as best they can.

II.32. शौच संतोष तपः स्वाध्यायेश्वर प्रणिधानानि नियमाः

śauca saṃtoṣa tapaḥ svādhyāya Īśvara praṇidhānāni niyamāḥ
"cleanliness, contentment, austerity/effort/heat, study, surrender to Īśvara, niyamas"

In this sūtra Patañjali lists the niyamas: the observances and attitudes
that yogīs should do, and have.

The niyamas are

- śauca – cleanliness
- saṃtoṣa – contentment
- tapas – effort/austerity
- svādhyāya – study
- Īśvara praṇidhāna – surrender to Īśvara

Śauca is cleanliness. You should keep yourself and your meditation
place clean. It's difficult to meditate if you are itchy due to fleas, dirt, etc. If
your mind isn't pure (contains arrogance, malice, conceit) you'll be afflicted
with unwanted thoughts. If your meditation space is messy you will have
problems meditating because you'll keep thinking that you need to clean it
up, or it will remind you of things that you need to do. Hariharānanda
mentions that alcohol removes control over the mind, and control of the mind
is what yogīs need to do, so alcohol should be avoided. He also mentions the
smell of putrid animal products, but that shouldn't be a problem anymore
with refrigeration.

Saṃtoṣa is contentment. Vācaspati Miśra says that contentment is the
absence of desire for more than the necessities required by life. Hariharānanda says that a yogī should think "what I have is enough." Hariharanada
also says that, to protect your feet from thorns, you only need to wear shoes,
and not to cover the face of the earth with leather, so happiness can be
derived from contentment and not from thinking "I shall be happy when I get
all I wish for." If you aren't concerned about the kind of car, the size of the
house, or the vacations that your neighbors go on, you can be content. This
doesn't mean that you shouldn't try to better yourself or your situation, but
limit what you are after to the necessities, not the nice-to-haves.

Tapas is austerity, effort, heat in your practice. It means that you need to work at it: it's not easy. Austerity can be pleasant or not depending on the situation. Hariharānanda focuses on tolerating hardship to become a yogī, but I think that there's more to it. See my comments on II.1 for more details on tapas.

Svadhyāya is study. Historically it referred to study of scripture and repeating mantras (japa). I think that it's valid to expand it a bit to the study of anything that will help lead to mokṣa.

Īśvara praṇidhāna is surrender to Īśvara. See my comments on II.1.

II.33. वितर्क बाधने प्रतिपक्ष भावनम्

vitarka bādhane pratipakṣa bhāvanam
"thoughts, being disturbed, opposite, cultivating"

If you are being disturbed by negative or unwanted thoughts, i.e. thoughts that are contrary to the yamas and niyamas, especially while meditating, you should cultivate thinking of opposite thoughts. Patañjali uses the words "pratipakṣa bhāvanam" for this. Bryant says that negative thoughts WILL occur and that, instead of beating yourself up over them, you should deal insightfully with them. Beating yourself up doesn't help, but sympathetically handling negative thoughts does. Patañjali wants the yogī to purify the mind by meditation and dealing with the obstacles of negative thoughts will help remove them from the mind, purifying the mind, thus making meditation fruitful.

II.34. वितर्का हिंसादयः कृत कारितानुमोदिता लोभ क्रोध मोह पूर्वका मृदु मध्याधिमात्रा दुःखाज्ञानानन्त फला इति प्रतिपक्ष भावनम्

vitarkāḥ hiṃsā ādayaḥ kṛta kārita anumoditāḥ lobha krodha moha pūr-
vakāḥ mṛdu madhya adhimātrāḥ duḥkha ajñāna ananta phalāḥ iti
pratipakṣa bhāvanam
"thoughts, harm, etc., performed, caused to be done, consented to,
greed, anger, delusion, preceded by, mild, medium, intense, suffering, ignorance, never-ending, fruit, then, opposite, cultivating"

Here Patañjali says that all thoughts and actions that harm, whether you do them yourself, cause someone else to do them, or you consent to them, are preceded by mild, medium, or intense greed, anger, or delusion, and result in the fruit of never-ending suffering and ignorance. Therefore you should think the opposite thoughts, as noted in the previous sūtra.

Negative thoughts and actions are yours whether you do them yourself, have someone else do them for you, or approve of them being done. So you can't absolve yourself of responsibility by saying that you didn't do it yourself. And these negative thoughts and actions result in suffering and ignorance.

Note that just thinking negative thoughts are karma; they cause a karmic result which will be experienced in the current, or a future, life.

II.35. अहिंसा प्रतिष्ठायां तत्सन्निधौ वैर त्यागः

ahiṃsā pratiṣṭhāyāṃ tat sannidhau vaira tyāgaḥ
"nonviolence, upon establishment, his, proximity/presence, hostility,
   abandonment"

In his pre-commentary before this sūtra, Vyāsa says that by doing prati-pakṣa bhāvanam (thinking the opposite thoughts), the negative thoughts fail to cause problems, and the yogī gets super-normal powers. These powers, which come from perfecting the yamas and niyamas, show the yogī's success. Sūtras 35-45 discuss these powers. Some of them are difficult to understand or to believe, but that's not the point. The point is that if you get any of these powers, you know that you are progressing.

In this sūtra, Patañjali says that when you have mastered ahiṃsā/non-violence/non-harming, all hostility ceases in your presence. Hariharānanda says that when you lose the desire to do harm or retaliate even when provoked, then you have mastered ahiṃsā.

II.36. सत्य प्रतिष्ठायां क्रियाफलाश्रयत्वम्

satya pratiṣṭhāyāṃ kriyā phala āśrayatvam
"truth, upon establishment, actions, fruits, the support of"

Here Patañjali says that when you have mastered truthfulness everything you say will become true. Hariharānanda says that if the yogī tells someone to be virtuous, a saṃskāra is activated in the person's mind and they become virtuous. He doesn't say if the yogī creates a new saṃskāra or simply activates an existing one. He also says that yogīs don't make statements that are beyond their power or will.

II.37. अस्तेय प्रतिष्ठायां सर्व रत्नोपस्थानम्

asteya pratiṣṭhāyāṃ sarva ratna upasthānam
"non-stealing, upon establishment, all, jewels, appear"

When you master non-stealing, all jewels/money/etc. come to you. This one says you don't have to worry about money if you perfect non-stealing.

A story by Swāmī Satchidānanda that I heard was that one time when he was broke, he entered a restaurant with a buffet line where the owner dished out food onto customer's plates. The Swāmī stood in the corner since he didn't have any money. The owner saw him and immediately said that he would serve Satchidānanda first, and for free. In *Autobiography of a Yogī*, Yogānanda mentioned that one time his guru told him to go to the town and spend the day with no money. Yogānanda said that he was worried about hunger but found out that people gave him food.

II.38. ब्रह्मचर्य प्रतिष्ठायां वीर्य लाभः

brahmacarya pratiṣṭhāyāṃ vīrya lābhaḥ

"celibacy, upon establishment, power, gaining"

The idea here is that you lose potency/power (vīrya) when you have sex. If you don't engage in sex, you will have more power to direct to other parts of your sādhana. Vyāsa says that a yogī that is firmly established in celibacy gets powers and siddhis that are mentioned in the third chapter. He also says that a person who is celibate can impart knowledge directly to disciples without talking (śaktipāta).

II.39. अपरिग्रह स्थैर्ये जन्म कथन्ता संबोधः

aparigraha sthairye janma kathantā saṃbodhaḥ

"non-acceptance, upon stability, births/incarnations, how and why, real-
    ization/knowledge"

This one is not obvious. Aparigraha means non-acceptance of more than necessary, or renunciation. Here, Patañjali says when you master non-accep-tance (aparigraha), you get the knowledge of your past and future births. Hariharānanda says it a bit differently: by meditating on the idea of the body as superfluous and insignificant, you get that knowledge. I haven't read any commentaries on this sūtra that fully make sense to me.

II.40. शौचात्स्वाङ्ग जुगुप्सा परैरसंसर्गः

śaucāt sva aṅga jugupsā paraiḥ asaṃsargaḥ

"cleanliness, one's own, limbs, disinterest/aversion/distaste, with others,
   non-contact"

By cleanliness, you develop disinterest/disgust/aversion/distaste for
your own body and the cessation of contact with others.

I frequently get the question of why the word 'jugupsā' is sometimes
translated by some commentators as 'disgust' when I'm lecturing on this
sūtra. According to the Apte Saṃskṛtam dictionary, the word has several
definitions: dislike, aversion, disgust, abhorrence. I checked four of my
regular commentaries and it's translated as distaste by Bryant, disinclination
by Vācaspati Miśra, aversion by Hariharānanda, disgust by Satchidānanda,
and aversion by Swāmī Bhārati. In another book by Zambito where he has 12
different translations of each sūtra, I see a few 'disgust' and some others too,
'indifference', 'shrinks from', 'gains distance'. So you can see that there are
quite a few different translations of the word. I prefer disinterest as opposed
to disgust.

As to why the yogī would have this attitude towards their own body, it
comes from the knowledge that the body is never pure, no matter how much
you clean it. If you get close enough and magnify the skin, you will always
find that it's not pure and clean. And the inside of the body is filled with
disgusting stuff like poop and other nasty things. So if the yogī knows this,
they will not be attracted to their own body – or any other bodies for that
matter. The yogī will keep the body clean, strong, and healthy because it's the
tool to attain mokṣa in this lifetime. But the yogī won't be attracted to it or
any other body.

There's a story that I like to tell my students about this sūtra. There was
a man that came to an āśrama and saw an incredibly beautiful yoginī. He was
so taken with her beauty that he asked her to marry him. She said that if he
went away and came back in a month and still wanted to marry her that she
would do it. He agreed and left for a month. During that month the yoginī
collected everything that came out of her body, pee, poop, snot, menses, etc.
and put it in a large bucket. When he returned after a month to marry her, she
gave him the bucket. He was appalled and disgusted by the contents of the
bucket and asked her what it was. She said that it all came out of her body,
and did he still want to marry her? He decided to become a yogī instead.

So the problem is what to do if you are attracted to your own body and others too? I always reply that if you are an advanced yogī, due to work in your current and previous lives, you won't be interested in having relationships, or sex, or anything like that. If you are attracted to yours and other bodies, you still have a way to go in your own sādhana.

But don't think that just because you want relationships or sex that it's bad, or that there's something wrong with you; you just haven't advanced enough in your sādhana yet. There is a place in society for people that aren't advanced yogīs; we need them to protect the country, farm the land, produce food, run businesses to keep society going, etc. We are all on the path, just at different points on that path.

But remember that Patañjali's method is to purify the body and the mind so that you can get to samādhi and therefore attain mokṣa, so śauca (cleanliness) also applies to the mind. If your mind is not pure you can't get to samādhi and get the viveka khyatiḥ (discriminative wisdom) you need to attain mokṣa. The word can also apply to your life and where you do your meditation. If your life is not pure, and you are meditating in a messy room, you will be distracted.

In the Bhagavad Gītā, VI.10 – VI.I2, Kṛṣṇa says "The yogī should concentrate constantly on the Self, remaining in solitude, alone, with controlled mind and body, having no desires and destitute of possessions. Establishing a firm seat for himself in a clean place, not too high, not too low, covered with a cloth, and antelope skin, and kuśa grass, there, having directed his mind to a single object, with his thought and the activity of the senses controlled, seating himself on the seat, he should practice yoga for the purpose of self-purification."

II.41 सत्त्व शुद्धि सौमनस्यैकाग्ग्येन्द्रिय जयात्म दर्शन योग्यत्वानि च

sattva śuddhi saumanasya ekāgrya indriya jaya ātma darśana yogyatvāni
ca

"sattva guṇa, purification, cheerfulness, one-pointedness, senses, conquering, self, view, fitness, and"

Here Patañjali is adds to the previous sūtra about physical cleanliness and its results. In this sūtra, he discusses mental cleanliness. He says that when you purify your mind, you become cheerful, one-pointed, and conquer your senses. When you do this you are fit to see your self/puruṣa. Remember though, that since the puruṣa is more subtle than the buddhi, it can't directly see the puruṣa, but can learn about it.

The reason mental purity is important, according to Vyāsa, is mental cleanliness leads to cheerfulness, which leads to one-pointedness, which leads to conquest of the senses, which leads to fitness for seeing the self.

Bhārati says that śauca (cleanliness) is not a negation of the physical self, but an affirmation of the spiritual self. Some people claim that yoga is a philosophy that practices body negation. But it's not. It's a way to use the body to get the knowledge needed to remove pain and attain mokṣa. Granted that in the end the body is gone because you are dead, but the idea is that you don't want to be reborn, and according to Patañjali you can't be liberated and alive, i.e. a jīvanmukta. See Appendix C for a discussion of jīvanmukti.

II.42 संतोषादनुत्तमः सुख लाभः

saṃtoṣāt anuttamaḥ sukha lābhaḥ
"contentment, unsurpassed, happiness, gain"

Vyāsa says that the pleasure from the world or in the celestial realms is much less than the happiness you get from mastering contentment, i.e. removing desires. Śrī Śrī Ravi Śaṅkar said "how can you have desires if you are content, and how can you be content if you have desires?" Patañjali is giving another reason to take up the yogic path here, the idea that you get unsurpassed happiness from following this niyama.

II.43 कायेन्द्रिय सिद्धिरशुद्धि क्षयात् तपसः

kāya indriya siddhiḥ aśuddhi kṣayāt tapasaḥ

"body, senses, perfection, impure, through elimination, austerity"

In this sūtra Patañjali is discussing the results of tapas. Patañjali says that by tapas you perfect the body and the senses, and remove impurities, which will help you get to samādhi and eventually attain mokṣa. Tapas tends to be translated as penance, but that's not really correct. In a yoga perspective it's putting effort, heat, in your practice. The best translation is austerity. See my comments on II.1 for more on tapas.

The word 'siddhiḥ' is translated as perfection. Vyāsa suggests that this means that you also get some of the siddhis, or powers, mentioned in the third chapter when you master austerity.

II.44 स्वाध्यायाद् इष्ट देवता संप्रयोगः

svādhyāyāt iṣṭa devatā samprayogaḥ

"from study, preferred, deity, connection"

In this sūtra Patañjali says that through svādhyāya (study) you get a connection to your preferred deity (iṣṭa devatā). Remember that svādhyāya is traditionally meant to be study of scripture and repeating of mantras (japa). In Hinduism we have the idea of your iṣṭa devatā, which is your preferred deity among all the Hindu deities. This can also be applied to Christians and Muslims, except that their choice is limited to one.

II.45 समाधि सिद्धिरीश्वर प्रणिधानात्

samādhi siddhiḥ Īśvara praṇidhānāt

"samādhi, perfection, Īśvara, from surrender"

This sūtra is associated with I.23 where Patañjali said that Īśvara praṇidhāna is an alternative method to get to samādhi. Here he says that by surrendering to Īśvara (most likely your iṣṭa devatā from the previous sūtra), Īśvara will give you samādhi.

Hariharānanda says that some ignorant people say that if by surrendering to Īśvara you can get samādhi, then the other limbs of Aṣṭāṅga Yoga are not needed. He says that this is not true and that samādhi implies doing all the eight limbs is required. Īśvara praṇidhāna just makes it easier and faster to get samādhi.

Bhārati points out that Vyāsa, in his comments on I.1, says that samādhi is a universal attribute of the mind. He goes on to say that samādhi only becomes manifest, as opposed to being created, when the yogī is ready, i.e. after doing the first seven limbs. But he doesn't say it's easy.

<u>Section Summary</u>

In this section Patañjali gives the yamas and niyamas (ethical restraints, and observances and attitudes), which are the first two limbs of his Aṣṭāṅga Yoga. He says that the yamas are a great vow and must be held at all times and places. Then, he gives results of perfecting each of them.

II.46 – II.55 Āsana, Prāṇāyāma, Pratyāhāra

In sūtras II.30 – II.45 Patañjali discussed the first two limbs of Aṣṭāṅga Yoga – yama and niyama – and the results of doing them. Now he spends the rest of the chapter discussing the next three limbs, āsana, prāṇāyāma, and pratyāhāra.

II.46 स्थिर सुखमं आसनम्

sthira sukhaṃ āsanam
"steady, comfortable, posture"

This is one of the most well known sūtras where Patañjali says that an āsana should be steady and comfortable. He only spends three sūtras out of 196 discussing āsana, only 1.5%, but we in the West tend to think that āsana 'is' yoga. There's a disconnect there. Many people that do yoga only do āsana practice and think that yoga is āsana, or they meditate and think that's yoga. Neither are correct. Yoga is a system that allows you to attain mokṣa. Āsana, meditation, and the six other limbs combined are yoga.

The purpose of āsana, all the various poses, is to give you a strong, healthy, flexible, body so you can be comfortable and not move while in meditation. According to Bhārati, an āsana needs to be stable, motionless, without trembling, not subject to agitation, easeful, and comfortable. He then says that only when the posture meets all these conditions is it an āsana according to Patañjali.

One argument that comes up frequently is what exactly is the definition of āsana? The dictionary says that it's 'to take a seat', and some people argue that āsana is therefore only sitting and meditating. However, the dictionary has a number of other definitions for āsana, e.g. halting, encamping, abiding, seat, position. The root word for āsana is 'as', which means, among other things: be, exist, happen, take place, dwell. So āsana means, in this context, more than just sitting. It means any posture that you can meditate in. Bryant mentions that the Hatha Yoga Pradipika speaks of 84 āsanas, and the Gorakṣa-śataka says that there are 8,400,000 āsanas!

Many of the ancient yogīs meditated standing up, and in other poses; there's a story about a demoness that meditated on Lord Śiva for 10,000 years while standing on one foot at the top of a mountain. Bryant mentions the story of Śiśupāla, who hated Kṛṣṇa so much that he couldn't think of anything else, and was therefore actually always meditating.

II.47 प्रयत्न शैतिल्यानन्त समापत्तिभ्याम्

prayatna śaitilya ananta samāpattibhyām
"effort, relaxation, the infinite, meditative from both (effort and relaxation)"

When āsana becomes relaxing and meditative, you have mastered āsana. This makes sense even though he doesn't say 'mastered āsana;' all the commentators agree with this. I sometimes say 'at some point the āsana disappears and the only thing left is you in a different shape.' Āsana practice, if practiced long enough, automatically becomes relaxing and meditative. An example that I like to use is a time when some of us 'advanced' students were doing our own practice in the back of the room while the teacher taught the other students in the front of the room. I happened to be right next to the stereo that the teacher was using for music during the class. After class the teacher asked me what I thought of the music, and I couldn't answer because I hadn't heard it during the entire time I was practicing because I was so deep into my practice that I wasn't aware of anything outside of me.

Āsana practice can be meditative, but not meditation, because your mind isn't still since it's focused on breathing during each āsana and then thinking about the next āsana as you move into it. It's meditative because your mind, while not still, is still very focused. However, if you stay in a single āsana, that can be meditation. Āsana practice also feels really good when you get accomplished at it. By accomplished I'm referring to the previous sūtra; āsana should be steady and comfortable. When you get to this point, the practice is a joy and you can't wait to do it again.

Fancy or very difficult āsanas don't get you to mokṣa, they just help keep the practice interesting, challenging, and fun. While I was recovering from rotator cuff surgery, I found that I got just as much, if not more, from the 'easy' poses as the 'difficult' ones. And remember that a pose that's easy for one person may be difficult to another person, and a pose that's easy for the other person may be difficult for the first person. Due to this I have given up the notion of 'difficult' and 'easy' poses, they are just poses.

II.48 ततो द्वन्द्वानभिघातः

tataḥ dvandva anabhighātaḥ
"then, pairs of opposites, not afflicted"

In II.46 Patañjali said that āsana should be steady and comfortable. In II.47 he said that you've mastered āsana when it becomes relaxing and meditative. In this sūtra he says that when you've mastered āsana you are unaffected by the pairs-of-opposites/dualities such as heat/cold, pleasure/pain. The point here is that you have transcended your bodily sensations and removed those distractions so that you can better meditate, that meditation is what you need to get samādhi, and then attain mokṣa.

II.49 तस्मिन् सति श्वास प्रश्वासयोर्गति विच्छेदः प्राणायामः

tasmin sati śvāsa prasvāsayoḥ gati vicchedaḥ prāṇa āyāmaḥ
"that, being, inhalation, exhalation, movement, breaking/interruption,
    prāṇa, expansion"

Patañjali says here that once ('that being') you have mastered āsana, prāṇāyāma (expansion of prāṇa) should be started. Patañjali says that prāṇāyāma is the breaking or interrupting the natural movement of your inhales and exhales.

He says that you shouldn't start prāṇāyāma until after you've mastered āsana, but that's not what is done currently. Hariharānanda, though, says that it's ok to do prāṇāyāma before mastering āsana if your body is steady and your mind is tranquil. I've heard that Kṛṣṇamacarya taught prāṇāyāma to children. Yoga teacher training programs teach it to the teacher trainees before they have mastered āsana.

Some people believe that the word prāṇāyāma means control of the breath. This is because they break the word up into two words – prāṇa and yama. This is not correct because the final 'a' in prāṇa is a short 'a' instead of a long 'aa' (ā). The proper way to break up the word is prāṇa and āyāma, which means expansion of prāṇa. So, with prāṇāyāma you are trying to increase the amount of prāṇa in your body. My teacher says that breath is not prāṇa, but prāṇa floats on the breath, which might be why prāṇāyāma is sometimes called breath control or breath work. See Appendix H for a discussion on what prāṇa is.

Prāṇāyāma also tends to, but not always, balance the main nadīs (energy channels), ida and piṅgala, so that your meditation is better; the sleepy ida nadī offsets the monkey-mind piṅgala nadī, because both nostrils are open and working. If you notice, most of the time only one of your nostrils is actually working and the other is not. Prāṇāyāma, especially nadī-śodhana (alternate nostril breathing) helps to open the closed side. Both nadīs start at the base of the spine and crisscross the spine up to the head where the ida nadī is associated with the left nostril and the piṅgala nadī with the right.

There are many types of prāṇāyāma which are beyond the scope of this work. One point that I would like to make though is that prāṇāyāma should be easy and comfortable. If it's not, stop and start over again, possibly doing fewer rounds. In kapālabhāti and bhastrikā prāṇāyāmas, most people start out with lots of movement in their belly and chest but as time goes on it becomes more and more subtle (mentioned in the next sūtra), your body is barely moving, but the effect is still the same.

II.50 बाह्याभ्यन्तर स्तम्भ वृत्तिः देश काल संख्याभिः परिदृष्टो दीर्घ सूक्ष्मः

bāhya ābhyantara stambha vṛttiḥ deśa kāla saṃkhyābhiḥ paridṛṣṭaḥ
    dīrgha sūkṣmaḥ
"external, internal, restrained, activity, place, time, number, observed,
    long, subtle"

Here Patañjali continues on from the previous sūtra, and says that prāṇāyāma includes inhaling, exhaling, and holding your breath. He says that when you do prāṇāyāma you focus on a place where each inhale or exhale can be felt, how long each inhale, exhale, or hold will be, and how many repetitions of the prāṇāyāma you will do. He also says that prāṇāyāma, over time, becomes long and subtle.

A point I would like to make here is that there are many different types of prāṇāyāma, and they should be learned from an experienced teacher. Patañjali doesn't mention any particular form or practice of prāṇāyāma, just like he doesn't mention which āsanas to do. This is between you and your teacher.

Prāṇa is very powerful and can therefore be dangerous. One day while I was meditating in a conference room at work, near the end of my meditation, it felt like a fire hose of prāṇa was stuck in my chest and turned on full blast. I thought that I was literally going to explode and splatter all over the walls. I asked Śiva (my iṣṭa devatā) to stop because I was scared, and it immediately stopped. The next day it happened again, but this time I thought that Śiva won't give me anything that I can't handle so I just sat there and took it. When my meditation timer went off, I literally staggered back down the hall to my desk and collapsed into my chair. I was completely drained and could barely walk to my desk.

II.51 बाह्याभ्यन्तर विषयाक्षेपी चातुर्तः

bāhya ābhyantara viśaya ākṣepī cāturtaḥ

"external, internal, scope, surpassing, the fourth"

Patañjali says that there is a fourth type of prāṇāyāma, which surpasses the scope of inhales and exhales. This means going beyond those two things by not breathing. In this case your breath just stops without any effort. Vyāsa says that the fourth is when your prāṇāyāma, controlling your inhales, exhales, and holding the breath, becomes so slow and subtle, over a long time, that your breath just stops. This is called kumbhaka.

II.52 ततः क्षीयते प्रकाशावरणम्

tataḥ kṣīyate prakāśa āvaraṇam

"then, diminishes, light, covering"

In this sūtra Patañjali gives the results of prāṇāyāma: the covering over the light of knowledge diminishes. Remember that his main idea in all the sūtras is to purify your mind and body so that you can meditate, get into samādhi, and then attain mokṣa. Here he's saying that there's a covering over the mind, and prāṇāyāma is like scrubbing off the layer of dirt over the mind and letting the light of knowledge shine through. When you have done this, you are closer to attaining mokṣa. Vyāsa says on this sūtra that there is no ascetic endeavor (tapas) that is better than prāṇāyāma.

II.53 धारणासु च योग्यता मनसः

dhāraṇāsu ca yogyatā manasaḥ
"concentration, and, fitness, mind"

Patañjali finishes up his discussion of prāṇāyāma with this sūtra, which says that when you've mastered prāṇāyāma your mind is fit for concentration (dhāraṇā III.1). There's only one more 'external' limb of yoga – pratyāhāra – before you get to the last three 'internal' limbs of his eight limbs of Aṣṭāṅga Yoga.

II.54 स्व विषयासम्प्रयोगे चित्तस्य स्वरुपानुकार इवेन्द्रियाणां

प्रत्याहारः

sva viṣaya asamprayoge cittasya svarūpa anukāraḥ iva indriyāṇāṃ
   pratyāharaḥ
"own, sense objects, non-conjunction, mind, nature, following, like, of
   the senses, withdrawal"

This sūtra introduces the fifth limb of Patañjali's eight limbs: pratyāhāra. When you are meditating you can't stop your ears from hearing, your nose from smelling, your skin feeling a breeze, etc. These are more distractions that you need to get rid of.

The citta is made up of three parts: buddhi (the discriminator), ahaṃkāra (ego), and manas (sensory input). The manas is connected to the sensory organs, which is what this limb is all about, i.e. you need to disconnect the manas from the buddhi so that sensory input is cut off. This is called pratyāhāra. As usual, Patañjali doesn't give any information on how this is to be done.

Vyāsa quotes the Praśna Upaniṣad: "as the bees follow in flight the queen bee who is fleeing, and then settle down as she settles down, so the senses come under control upon the mind-field becoming controlled." He's indicating that when you calm your mind from prāṇāyāma, pratyāhāra automatically comes. Hariharānanda says that the senses follow the mind so if the mind is on an external object that's where the senses go, but if it's focused internally and is not moving then the senses stop.

II.55 ततः परमा वश्यतेन्द्रियाणाम्

tataḥ paramā vaśyatā indriyāṇām

"then, highest, control, of the senses"

If you master pratyāhāra then you have the highest control of the senses and can get rid of the distractions from them. Vyāsa says that pratyāhāra is complete disconnection from sense objects, not just ones that are prohibited, or sense experiences without attachment.

Section Summary

In this section Patañjali finishes up his discussion of the first five limbs of Aṣṭāṅga Yoga. He defines āsana (physical postures) as steady and comfortable, how to know when you've mastered this limb (when āsana becomes relaxing and meditative), and then says that you transcend the effects of bodily sensations when you have mastered it. Next, he defines and discusses prāṇāyāma (expanding prāṇa in your body), and says that when you master this limb, the covering over the light of knowledge diminishes so that you get closer to attaining mokṣa. He finishes the section by discussing pratyāhāra (sense withdrawal), which removes distractions from sensory input so that it's easier to get to samādhi and attain mokṣa.

Chapter Summary

In this second chapter, he first discusses Kriyā Yoga (the first three things you tell a new student to do) then the five kleśas/obstacles/afflictions that keep you from attaining mokṣa. After that, he spends three sūtras on karma. Then he discusses that the reason to take up the yogic path is due to pain and some high-level information on what we are doing and why. He finishes up the chapter with a discussion of the yamas and niyamas, and their results, followed by āsana, prāṇāyāma, and pratyāhāra. In the next chapter, he finishes up discussing the last three limbs, and discusses the super-normal powers that you can get from meditation and some final information about them.

Vibhūti Pāda

III.1 – III.12 Dhāraṇā, Dhyāna, Samādhi, Pariṇāmas

Patañjali has discussed the goal of yoga and various topics about samādhi and mokṣa in the first chapter, and Kriyā Yoga, kleśas, karma, an overview on what we're doing, and the first five limbs of his Aṣṭāṅga Yoga in the second chapter. In the third chapter he discusses the last three limbs of yoga, powers/siddhis/attainments, and more on mokṣa.

In this section he gives his definitions for concentration (dhāraṇā), meditation (dhyāna), and a special, very deep kind of meditation (samādhi), followed by some additional sūtras about them. There's no good English word for samādhi. In sūtras III.9 – III.12 he discusses the pariṇāmas, which are the transformations (pariṇāmas) of the mind that happen over time when you consistently work on your concentration (dhāraṇā) practice, in an effort to get to meditation (dhyāna). The transformations are 1) nirodha – increase in saṃskāras that promote meditation, 2) samādhi – decrease in the number of objects your mind wanders to during meditation, and 3) ekāgrata – increase in the probability that the incoming thought is the same as the outgoing thought during dhāraṇā.

A common misconception is that meditation is emptying your mind, but that's incorrect. You're mind cannot be empty. There is always a thought in your mind. What you are really trying to do is to still the fluctuations of the mind

Patañjali, in I.2 said that yoga is stilling the fluctuations of the citta/mind. However, Bryant, in his commentary on III.12, points out that your mind is never perfectly still due to the guṇas (the qualities of prakṛti), which are always changing, so the contents of your mind continually have an outgoing thought, followed immediately by an incoming thought. He uses the metaphor of a movie projector showing a scene where nothing changes. As far as we can tell there is only one, unchanging picture projected on the wall. But it's really a large number of identical pictures moving past the projector's light. To continue the metaphor, as a picture starts to come in front of the light, it's an incoming thought. As it starts to move past the light, it's an outgoing thought.

While Patañjali doesn't use the description of stilling the mind in the next three sūtras, he uses the contents of the mind to define concentration (dhāraṇā), and meditation (dhyāna), which is another way to say it. If all the pictures on the film are the same the mind is 'still'. If the pictures are different the mind is wandering/fluctuating (not still). He then defines samādhi as meditation (dhyāna) with an extra characteristic which will be discussed in III.3.

III.1 देश बन्धश्चित्तस्य धारणा

deśa bandhaḥ cittasya dhāraṇā
"place, fixed/bound, of the mind, concentration"

Dhāraṇā is what most of us think of as meditation. But it isn't. It's concentration, or pre-meditation. In this limb you are trying to fix your mind on a single object (the one-pointed mind).

But in dhāraṇā the thought in your mind keeps changing. Using the movie projector metaphor, the pictures on the film are not the same: they change. The incoming thought isn't always the same as the outgoing thought. This can also be expressed as a wandering mind.

Most of us remain in this level for a very long time – many years, so don't give up if you are working for years in concentration (dhāraṇā), trying to get to meditation (dhyāna), which is discussed in the next sūtra

III.2 तत्र प्रत्ययैक तानता ध्यानम्

tatra pratyaya eka tānatā dhyānam
"there, thought/idea, one, uninterrupted, meditation"

In this sūtra Patañjali gives his definition of actual meditation (dhyāna), as different from dhāraṇā. In dhāraṇā, as I mentioned, the incoming thought is not necessarily the same as the outgoing thought, and you have to continue to bring your mind back to your object of meditation. Meditation (dhyāna) is when the incoming thought is always the same as the outgoing thought – for as long as you want. He says that dhyāna is when there is one uninterrupted thought in your mind.

III.3 तद् एवार्थ मात्र निर्भासं स्व रूप शून्यं इव समाधिः

tad eva artha mātra nirbhāsaṃ sva rūpa śūnyaṃ iva samādhiḥ

"that, just, object, alone, shining, own, nature, absent, as if, samādhi"

In this sūtra Patañjali gives his definition of samādhi: it's when just the object of meditation alone is shining, and the mind ('that' in the sutra), is as if its nature is absent. The difference between samādhi and dhyāna (meditation) is that when in dhyāna you are aware of "I am meditating on that. In samādhi the "I am meditating" disappears, and the only thing in your mind is the object of meditation. Samādhi is a very deep dhyāna (meditation), but your focus is the same since you need to go through dhyāna every time to get to samādhi. This is a different way to express his definition in I.41 where he said that the mind becomes colored by the object of meditation, just like a clear crystal takes on the color of whatever cloth it is resting on.

The difference between dhāraṇā, dhyāna, and samādhi is as follows. In dhāraṇā (concentration) the contents of your mind changes. In dhyāna (meditation) the contents of your mind don't change, in samādhi you lose the awareness of meditating on an object and are aware only of the object of meditation. You always have to go through dhāraṇā, and dhyāna, to get to samādhi, but your object is the same in all three. The term Patañjali uses for doing all three consecutively is saṃyama (III.4).

You can do dhāraṇā without dhyāna, and dhyāna without samādhi. However, you can't do samādhi without doing dhyāna first, and you can't do dhyāna without doing dhāraṇā first.

In samādhi you focus on the various levels of the Sāṃkhya devolution tree until you get the discriminative wisdom (viveka khyātih) that you need to get into asamprajñāta samādhi (samādhi without an object of meditation) (I.18 and I.51) and then attain mokṣa. See my comments on I.18 for information on how this works. From samādhi, at some point you completely know everything about the object you are focusing on (see my comments on I.18), the next time you meditate you do saṃyama (dhāraṇā, dhyāna, and samādhi in succession) on something in the next level up in the Sāṃkhya devolution tree. The idea is that you keep focusing on more and more subtle things until you get the discriminative wisdom (viveka khyātih) of the difference between puruṣa and prakṛti.

Some people think that meditating and getting into samādhi is easy. I've had runners say that they are meditating while running, but this is not meditation or samādhi because their mind isn't still: it's paying attention to where to place the feet, avoiding obstacles, and making sure that they take the correct turns at the appropriate times. I've heard of one person who said that they were in samādhi during a car accident because all they could think of during the accident was the accident. This is also incorrect because samādhi and meditation are intentional and have the purpose of attaining mokṣa. In an accident you aren't intentionally focusing on the accident as a way to attain mokṣa. I have also heard it said that samādhi is a 'natural' state of the mind and is therefore easy, which is also incorrect because the nature of the mind is not to be still. The nature of the manas is to continually receive sense input, process it, and pass it on to the buddhi, whose nature is to process the inputs from the manas. In yoga we are attempting to still the mind (yogaś citta vṛtti nirodhaḥ) (I.2), which if you've tried it, you will know is very difficult.

In this sūtra Patañjali only gives his definition of samādhi. He gave information as to what you are supposed to be doing while in samādhi in the first chapter. Next he gives some more sūtras on these limbs and then discusses the changes/transformations (pariṇāmas) to the mind after doing dhāraṇā for a long time.In most of the rest of this chapter he discusses the siddhis/super-normal powers that you can get from samādhi. However, he also says, in III.37, that the siddhis are an obstacle to samādhi.

III.4 त्रयं एकत्र संयमः

trayam ekatra samyamaḥ

"three, together, samyama"

In this sūtra Patañjali is defining a short-cut word, samyama, to use so he doesn't have to continually say "doing dhāraṇā, dhyāna, and samādhi...". The dictionary definition of the word is the combination of the last three limbs of Patañjali's Aṣṭāṅga Yoga. In many of the sūtras in this chapter he says 'by doing samyama on x ...'

One point here is that when you, as an advanced meditator that can actually get into samādhi, sit down to meditate, you start by focusing your mind on a single object (dhāraṇā), then when your mind is not changing you get into dhyāna, and finally samādhi.

III.5 तज्जयात् प्रज्ञालोकः

tat jayāt prajñā ālokaḥ
"that, mastery, wisdom/knowledge, light"

Here Patañjali says that the more you master saṃyama (dhāraṇā, followed by dhyāna, followed by samādhi), the more you get the light of discriminative wisdom (viveka khyātiḥ). This goes along with the main theme in the book that you attain mokṣa from discriminative wisdom, which you get from samādhi, which is a form of meditation.

III.6 तस्य भूमिषु विनियोगः

tasya bhūmiṣu viniyogaḥ
"its, on the levels, application"

Here Patañjali continues on with his discussion of saṃyama. He says that you need to apply saṃyama to the various levels of samprajñāta samādhi discussed in the first chapter: vitarka, vicāra, ānanda, and asmitā (I.17, and I.41 – I.45). Vyāsa says that you have to go through the various levels in the order they were presented in the first chapter, and that you can't skip any levels. There are no shortcuts except through Īśvara praṇidhāna where Īśvara's grace will help you get to samādhi as noted in II.45. He also notes that through Īśvara's grace you may skip some levels, and the lower levels are automatically acquired if you skip some in this way.

Vyāsa quotes an old saying here: "Yoga is to be known by Yoga, and Yoga itself leads to Yoga. He who remains steadfast in Yoga always delights in it."

III.7 त्रयमन्तरङ्गं पूर्वेभ्यः

trayam antar aṅgaṃ pūrvebhyaḥ

"three, internal, limb, than the preceding"

In this sūtra Patañjali says that the last three limbs of yoga (dhāraṇā, dhyāna, and samādhi) are internal, as opposed to the first five limbs (yama, niyama, āsana, prāṇāyāma, and pratyāhāra). This makes sense since the first 4 limbs are outwardly perceivable by looking at the yogī's actions, and they consist mainly of bodily actions. Pratyāhāra (the fifth limb) is also more external because it's about shutting off external sensory input. These last three limbs are all focused inwards to the mind, even though you may be doing saṃyama on an external object.

III.8 तद् अपि बहिरङ्गं निर्बीजस्य

tad api bahir aṅgaṃ nirbījasya

"that, even, external, limbs, to the seedless"

Continuing from the previous sūtra, Patañjali says that the practice of the three parts of saṃyama (dhāraṇā, dhyāna, and samprajñāta samādhi) is external to asamprajñāta (seedless) samādhi. This is because saṃyama is all about prakṛti, which is external to the puruṣa, and there's no prakṛti in asamprajñāta samādhi because at that point prakṛti is separated from puruṣa and doesn't exist for the puruṣa anymore (see I.51 and II.25).

III.9 व्युत्थान निरोध संस्कारयोरभिभव प्रादुर्भावौ निरोध क्षण चित्तान्वयो निरोध परिणामः

vyutthāna nirodha saṃskārayoḥ abhibhava prādurbhāvau nirodha kṣaṇa
    citta anvayaḥ nirodha pariṇāmaḥ
"outgoing, restraining, mental impressions, disappearance, appearance,
    restraining, moment, mind, conjunction, suppression, transforma-
    tion"

This sūtra is the first of four that discuss the transformations of the mind during concentration (dhāraṇā). The first transformation is called the nirodha pariṇāma, or restraining transformation. During dhāraṇā, the contents of your mind change. This is caused by the anti-meditation (outgoing) saṃskāras, while the pro-meditation (restraining) saṃskāras want to keep you in dhāraṇā, moving towards dhyāna.

This sūtra says that, over time, the pro-meditation saṃskāras get stronger and the anti-meditation ones get weaker. This transformation is the nirodha pariṇāma. In essence, the pro-meditation saṃskāras overpower the anti-meditation ones, and therefore the time that your mind is in dhāraṇā becomes longer.

III.10 तस्य प्रशान्त वाहिता संस्कारात्

tasya praśānta vāhitā saṃskārāt
"its, calm, flow, from mental impressions"

Patañjali says that the calm flow of the mind comes from the pro-meditation saṃskāras that you get from dhāraṇā, which get stronger over time and overcome the outgoing saṃskāras. So, instead of having waves like in the ocean, you have a smooth flow like a river.

III.11 सर्वार्थतैकाग्रतयोः क्षयोदयौ चित्तस्य समाधि परिणामः

sarva arthatā eka agratayoḥ kṣaya udayau cittasya samādhi pariṇāmaḥ
"all, objects, one, object, destruction, rise, of the mind, samādhi, transformation"

Here Patañjali gives the second pariṇāma (transformation). He says that, over time, there is a transformation that is the weakening (destruction) of the tendency of focusing on all objects, and the strengthening (rise) of the tendency of focusing on a single object. This is the samādhi pariṇāma. The name samādhi pariṇāma, is confusing, and I don't understand why he picked it.

In dhāraṇā, the contents of your mind are changing, but due to the samādhi pariṇāma, the transformation is getting you closer to dhyāna. The incoming thought tends to be from a smaller and smaller number of different thoughts, until it gets down to one, which is discussed in the next sūtra. Using the movie projector metaphor, the number of different pictures on the entire film decreases.

III.12 ततः पुनः शान्तोदितौ तुल्य प्रत्ययौ चित्तस्यैकाग्रता

परिणामः

tataḥ punaḥ śānta uditau tulya pratyayau cittasya eka agratā pariṇāmaḥ
"then, again, subsiding, rising, the same, thought, of the mind, one, object, transformation"

This is the last sūtra on the three pariṇāmas. Patañjali says that, over time, as you are in concentration (dhāraṇā) and working to get to meditation (dhyāna), the length of time that the incoming thought is the same as the outgoing thought is lengthening. This is the ekāgrata pariṇāma. Using the movie projector metaphor again, the number of identical pictures in a row on the film, before you get a different picture, goes up. When the incoming thought is always the same as the outgoing thought, you are in dhyāna.

An important thing to remember here is that your mind can't be empty. There is always a thought there.

<u>Section Summary</u>

In this section Patañjali defines the final three limbs of his Āṣṭāṅga Yoga: dhāraṇā (concentration), dhyāna (meditation), and samādhi. (a special, very deep meditation) Then he defines the term, saṃyama, that he uses to note that you need to do all three in succession when you sit down to meditate and get to samādhi.

The section ends with a discussion of the three pariṇāmas: 1) nirodha pariṇāma – over time your saṃskāras that keep the contents of your mind from changing gradually overpower the saṃskāras that keep the contents of your mind changing, 2) samādhi pariṇāma – over time your mind will tend to focus on fewer and fewer objects, tending towards one object/thought, and 3) ekāgrata pariṇāma – the incoming thought tends to be same as the outgoing thought when in dhāraṇā.

III.13 – III.15 Characteristics of Prakṛti

So far in this chapter Patañjali has discussed the last three limbs of Aṣṭāṅga Yoga: dhāraṇā, dhyāna, and samādhi. He spends most of the rest of this chapter on the siddhis, or super-normal powers, that you can get from samādhi. At the end of the chapter he presents more information on how to attain mokṣa.

But before Patañjali gets to the powers (siddhis), he spends a few sūtras discussing some esoteric aspects of prakṛti. These are necessary to be able to understand the powers.

III.13 एतेन भूतेन्द्रियेषु धर्म लक्षणावस्था परिणामा व्याख्याताः

etena bhūta indriyeṣu dharma lakṣaṇa avasthā pariṇāmāḥ vyākhyātāḥ
"by this, gross object, the senses, characteristics/form, temporal state,
condition, transformation, are described"

In this sūtra Patañjali discusses three types of changes to material objects: changes in characteristics, temporal changes, and changes of state.

The first change is changes in characteristics/form. These are changes from one form to another. The examples given are clay (soft, malleable) to a pot (single fixed form and hard) to potsherds (small irregular hard pieces), or a gold necklace that is melted down and turned into a ring. The underlying material stays the same, i.e. the first three are all basically clay and the second two are basically gold.

The next change is temporal change and relates to when an object exists/existed: past, present, and future. The pot may or may not have existed in the past, present, or the future. If it existed in the past, it might not exist in the present or the future. The same applies to the pot and the future.

The third change is a change of state. A shirt may have been new in the past, but in the present it may be old, or it may not be old until the future.

One thing to note here is that changes in characteristics are the only one that changes the form, color, texture of an object. Temporal changes and changes of state do not, at least mostly.

Vyāsa says that in all three type of changes the underlying 'stuff' doesn't change. It's still the same 'stuff'.

Patañjali discusses the types of changes to explain his definition of prakṛti as well as to distinguish his philosophy's definition of gross matter from the definition of other philosophies. He accepts the Sāṃkhya idea of satkāryavāda, which basically says that nothing is ever created (conservation of matter), things just change based on their characteristics. A common statement about this is that the effect is in the cause, which means that you can change milk into yogurt but not a pot.

III.14 शान्तोदिताव्यपदेश्य धर्मानुपाती धर्मी

śānta udita avyapadeśya dharma anupātī dharmī

"past, present, future, characteristics, follows, possessor of the characteristics"

In the previous sūtra Patañjali introduced three types of changes to gross matter: characteristics, temporal, and new-to-old. Now he's talking about temporal changes from future to the present to the past. Clay may in the future be made into a pot, and once the pot has been made it's in the present. Later, after the pot is broken into pieces and is maybe just dust, it's in the past. He's saying that while prakṛti, the possessor of characteristics, in the form of an object, can go through temporal changes, it's still just prakṛti.

Everything, except puruṣa, exists in either manifest or unmanifest form in prakṛti, and yogīs can manipulate prakṛti. <u>Manipulating prakṛti is an assumption in this philosophy:</u> gross matter is just a devolution of the subtle prakṛti that the buddhi is made of, and since yogīs can manipulate their buddhi, they can therefore manipulate devolutes from the buddhi.

In this sūtra Patañjali is using a different definition of 'dharma' than the usual one. Here the definition is characteristics. Therefore, the dharmī is the possessor of the characteristics.

III.15 क्रमान्यत्वं परिणामान्यत्वे हेतुः

krama anyatvaṃ pariṇāma anyatve hetuḥ

"sequence, change, transformation, in change, cause"

Continuing from the previous sūtra, here Patañjali says that the sequence (krama) of changes is the cause of the transformational changes of an object. Vyāsa, says that all three types of change (III.13) (characteristics, temporal, and state) are meant here. Remember that everything is always changing due to the fluctuations of the guṇas. An object such as clay goes through a sequence of characteristics from clay to a pot, to dust, and also goes through temporal changes from future to present to past. It also goes through changes due in state (new to old).

Vyāsa says that when the properties of an object (dharma from the previous sūtra) are seen by the yogī as the same as prakṛti (dharmi from the previous sūtra), then everything is called prakṛti (dharma) and the sequence of changes of an object are just sequences of changes of prakṛti.

Section Summary

In this section Patañjali expounds on prakṛti and changes to it, so as to set the stage for the sūtras on the powers that take up most of the rest of this chapter: powers that are basically manipulation of prakṛti. There are three types of changes: changes in characteristics/form, temporal (past, present, future), and change in state (new to old).

III.16 – III.48 Super-normal Powers

In this section Patañjali discusses the siddhis/super-normal powers that you can get from samādhi. While these powers may seem incredible, Bryant has an excellent discussion of this where he says that there are no texts that state that the powers listed are not true, and in fact they support the existence of them. He goes on to discuss that the powers are all basically manipulation of prakṛti, and since the yogi can manipulate prakṛti as discussed in III.13 – III.15, these powers make sense in the context of Sāṃkhya and Yoga metaphysics. So we will do what he suggests and assume that the siddhis are true and just try to understand what they are. Since these powers are disruptions of material nature, they disturb the natural order of things, and therefore yogīs won't use them because, first, they disrupt the natural order, and second, and most important, they are prakṛti, not the puruṣa (the real you), and are therefore uninteresting.

<u>A very important point to remember is that while these are amazing powers, in III.37 Patañjali says that they are an impediment to samādhi.</u> It's easy for a yogī that gets them to become attached to them and fall off the yogic path. I think that he mostly gives these here so that you know that they are normal and that you aren't going crazy if you get some of them. What would you think if you started levitating during meditation? I prefer to think of them as signposts that you are still making progress on your path, and should be noted and then ignored.

III.16 परिणाम त्रय संयमदतीतानागत ज्ञानम्

parināma traya saṃyamāt atīta anāgata jñānam
"transformation, three, from saṃyama, past, future, knowledge"

This is the first time that Patañjali uses his shortcut, saṃyama, to describe going through dhāraṇā, dhyāna, and to samādhi when meditating (see III.4 – III.6). He says that doing saṃyama on the transformations you get knowledge of the past and the future.

All Indian texts assume that the siddhis are true. None say that they are fake. They are a reasonable outcome from Sāṃkhya metaphysics. Since the bhūtas (gross matter) are an outcome of the tanmātras (subtle matter), and the tanmātras are an outcome of the ahaṃkāra (ego), which is an outcome of the buddhi, which comes from pradhāna (primordial matter), once a yogī completely controls their buddhi, it's reasonable that the siddhis are true. So, as I said above, we will suspend our skepticism and assume that they are a consequence of the fact that the buddhi is higher up on the Sāṃkhya devolution tree. Note that Patañjali never even tries to justify the existence or believability of the siddhis.

Meteorologists and economists predict the future based on past and current conditions. This siddhi is something like that. This also ties into the idea of satkāryavāda, that all effects are in their source, e.g. clay dust is inherent in the pot, and the pot is inherent in the clay.

III.17 शब्दार्थ प्रत्ययानामितरेतराध्यासात्सङ्करस्तत्प्रविभाग संयमात्सर्व भूत रुत ज्ञानम्

śabda artha pratyayānām itaretara adhyāsāt saṅkaraḥ tat pravibhāga
    saṃyamāt sarva bhūta ruta jñānam
"word, meaning, of the concept, each with the other, overlapping, com-
    mingling, their, distinctions, from saṃyama, all, beings, sounds,
    knowledge/speech"

Here Patañjali says that when you do saṃyama on the difference between a word, meaning (the object represented by the word), and a concept about the word (existing knowledge or prior experience) you get knowledge of all languages. Usually we don't distinguish between these three things, but when we hear a sound, we translate it to a word, and associate it with any existing knowledge (concepts) from the word. For example, when we hear the sound 'horse', we translate the sound to the word horse, and bring into our mind any existing knowledge (concepts) we have about horses.

Patañjali subscribes to the idea of 'sphota,' which assumes that the meaning is a separate entity from the sound of the word. This is opposed to the idea of 'varṇa vada' where the meaning is embedded in the individual sounds of the word. Sphota makes sense in that each language may have a different set of sounds to indicate the idea of a horse.

Hariharānanda says that the yogī can trace the sounds back to the vocal chords of the speaker, and from there into the speaker's mind.

III.18 संस्कार साक्षात्करणात्पूर्व जाति ज्ञानम्

saṃskāra sākṣāt karaṇāt pūrva jāti jñānam

"mental impression, visibly, causing, previous, birth, knowledge"

All actions are recorded in saṃskāras in your mind. Therefore, when you bring them into your perception (making them visible), by doing saṃyama on them, you get knowledge of previous births. You get to see the saṃskāras from previous lives, which gives you information about those lives.

Vyāsa tells the story of Jaigīṣavya, who got the knowledge of his previous births and was asked by Āvaṭya whether he enjoyed births as a celestial or human the best. He said they were all pain. Then Āvaṭya asked if his mastery over prakṛti and the unsurpassable pleasure of contentment was among his sorrows. He replied that the pleasure of contentment is superior to other enjoyments, but it is nothing but pain compared to the bliss of mokṣa, due to being free from the guṇas. The state of desire is from the guṇas and should be avoided.

III.19 प्रत्ययस्य पर चित्त ज्ञानम्

pratyayasya para citta jñānam

"of the ideas, other, mind, knowledge"

Here Patañjali says that from other's ideas, you can get knowledge of their thoughts. There is disagreement among the commentators on this one. According to Bryant, Vācaspati Miśra and Bhoja Rāja think that you meditate on the content/ideas of other's mind (pratyaya). Vijñānabhikṣu and Hariharānanda think that you need to meditate on your own mind, and then you can get the contents/ideas of the minds of others.

III.20 न च तत् सालम्बनं तस्याविषयीभूतत्वात्

na ca tat sa ālambanaṃ tasya avisayī bhūtatvat

"not, and, that, with, support, of that, not an object, because of being"

Patañjali is adding some clarification to the previous sūtra here. He says that you only get the ideas/thoughts about the object in another's mind because only the thoughts about the object are in that person's mind, and not the object itself.

The numbering of the following sūtras may be confusing if you have Vācaspati Miśra's commentary because he doesn't have this sūtra.

III.21 काय रूप संयमात्तद्ग्राह्य शक्ति स्तम्भे चक्षुः प्रकाशासंप्रयोगेऽन्तर्धानम्

kāya rūpa saṃyamāt tad grāhya śakti stambhe cakṣuḥ prakāśa
   asaṃprayoge antardhānam

"body's, form, from saṃyama, that, graspable, power, on the suspen-
   sion, eye, light, on the absence of contact, invisibility"

By doing saṃyama on the body's form you can become invisible. Vyāsa says that this also pertains to hearing (you can't be heard by someone else), etc. Most of the commentators don't talk about how this is done, but Vācaspati Miśra says by manipulating the tanmātras (subtle matter) you can do it.

III.21a एतेन शब्दाद्यन्तर्धानमुक्तम्

etena śabda ādi antardhānam uktam

"this, sound, and others, invisibility, addressed"

There are a number of commentaries that don't have this sūtra, so the numbering, after this, in some of the books will be off by one or two depending on which book you are looking at. I'm renumbering this one as III.21a to stay in line with most of the commentaries.

This sūtra just says what Vyāsa addressed in the previous sūtra where he said that that sūtra also applies to the other senses, hearing, etc. It appears that this was added to address the other senses, in some versions, but in other versions, Vyāsa addressed this in the previous sūtra, thus making this one superfluous, and indicates that it's been added later.

III.22 सोपक्रमं निरुपक्रमं च कर्म तत्संयमादपरान्त ज्ञानमरिष्टेभ्यो वा

sa upakramaṃ nir upakramaṃ ca karma tat saṃyamāt aparānta jñānam
    ariṣṭebhyaḥ vā

"with, approaching, without, approaching, and, action, that, from
    saṃyama, death, knowledge, from omens/signs/portents, or"

In this siddhi, Patañjali says that by doing saṃyama on karma you get knowledge of your death. He also says that you can get it by omens/signs/portents. When you meditate on karma you get knowledge of which ones are close to fruition (in this life) and which ones aren't (will come to fruition in a later life). By this knowledge you know how much more karma you have left to experience in this life, and therefore when you will die.

There are three types of karma: sañcita, prārabdha, āgāmin. Sañcita is all the karma that you have done in the past that you haven't yet received the results of. Prārabdha is the karma whose fruit you will experience in the current life. Āgāmin is the karma you have done in your current life but will get the fruit of in a later life. Some people add a fourth type, called kriya-māṇa, which is karma where you are getting the fruit of right now or in the very immediate future.

Karma is why suicide is fruitless. If you kill yourself before you have experienced the fruit of all of your prārabdha karma you'll just have to experience it in the next life.

III.23 मैत्र्यादिषु बलानि

maitrī ādiṣu balāni
"friendliness, etc., strength"

Here Patañjali says that by doing saṃyama on friendliness, you strengthen your feelings of friendliness. This applies to other feelings too. Refer to I.33 for the other feelings. He's just adding onto that sūtra. Note that you can't meditate on dispassion/non-attachment because that's an absence of a feeling, not a feeling.

III.24 बलेषु हस्ति बलादीनि

baleṣu hasti bala ādīni
"strength, elephant, strength, etc."

If you do saṃyama on the strength of an elephant you get the strength of an elephant. This can also be extended to be that if you meditate on the strength of anything you get that strength. Since gross matter is a derivative of subtle matter, and the yogī can affect it, this can be done, but the commentators don't say how.

III.25 प्रवृत्त्यालोक न्यासात्सूक्ष्म व्यवहित विप्रकृष्ट ज्ञानम्

pravṛtti āloka nyāsāt sūkṣma vyavahita viprakṛṣṭa jñānam
"cognition, light, directing, subtle, concealed, remote, knowledge"

In this sūtra, Patañjali states another assumption of the philosophy: the citta (mind), which consists of buddhi, ahaṃkāra, and manas, is all pervasive and infinite, and because of this you can get knowledge subtle, concealed, and remote objects, by directing the light of cognition at them, i.e. by thinking about them. However, you need to get rid of all of your rajas (heat, activity) and tamas (dull, static) guṇas (qualities of prakṛti) first.

Note that you don't do this siddhi by meditating. At some point the yogī's mind is so powerful and so sattvic that just by directing their mind, they can do this.

III.26 भुवन ज्ञानं सूर्ये संयमात्

bhuvana jñānaṃ sūrye samyamāt
"world, knowledge, sun, from samyama"

By doing samyama on the sun you get knowledge of the world. Vyāsa says that you get knowledge of all the celestial realms and goes into great detail about them. Some commentators say that you get knowledge of worlds, some say just the world, some say the solar system, some say subtle realms. Some commentators think that you need to meditate on the actual sun, while Vyāsa, Hariharānanda and Vācaspati Miśra think that you need to meditate on the solar entrance to the body, which Hariharānanda says is somewhere in the suṣumnā nadī (one of the subtle energy channels). So there's no consensus on this one.

III.27 चन्द्रे तारा व्यूह ज्ञानम्

candre tārā vyūha jñānam
"on the moon, stars, knowledge"

By doing samyama on the moon you get knowledge of solar systems. The commentators don't say anything here.

III.28 ध्रुवे तद् गति ज्ञानम्

dhruve tad gati jñānam
"on the pole star, their, movement, knowledge"

By doing samyama on the north star you get knowledge of the movements of the stars.

III.29 नाभि चक्रे काय व्यूह ज्ञानम्

nābhi cakre kāya vyūha jñānam
"navel, circular depression, body, arrangement, knowledge"

By doing saṃyama on the circular depression of the navel you get knowledge of the arrangement of the body. Cakra here has nothing to do with cakras in kuṇḍalinī or other related philosophies. It's just a place, a circular depression, in the body, i.e. the navel.

III.30 कण्ठ कूपे क्षुत्पिपासा निवृत्तिः

kaṇtha kūpe kṣut pipāsā nivṛttiḥ
"throat, pit/well, hunger, thirst, cessation"

By doing saṃyama on the pit of the throat you get rid of hunger and thirst.

III.31 कूर्म नाड्यां स्थैर्यं

kūrma nāḍyāṃ sthairyaṃ
"tortoise, nadī, steadiness"

By doing saṃyama on the subtle tortoise nadī (a subtle energy channel in your body), you get steadiness, and according to Vyāsa, can be still like a snake or alligator. Vyāsa says that the kūrma nadī is in the chest below the pit of the throat. Hariharānanda says that if you still your body you can still your mind.

III.32 मूर्ध ज्योतिषि सिद्ध दर्शनम्

mūrdha jyotiṣi siddha darśanam
"head, on light, perfected, vision"

By doing saṃyama on the light in the head, you get the vision of the siddhas, which are perfected beings that exist in the higher realms. They are sometimes called devas. The spot to focus on is the brahma-randhra, which is a place at the top of the head where an effulgent light shines.

III.33 प्रातिभाद्वा सर्वम्

prātibhāt vā sarvam
"from intuition, also, everything"

Here Patañjali says that you can also get knowledge of everything from intuition instead of just from viveka khyātiḥ. Patañjali discusses intuition more in III.35, III.36, and III.54. Intuition is a state of knowledge, and not acquired by saṃyama. By definition, intuition is spontaneous.

III.34 हृदये चित्त संवित्

hṛdaye citta saṃvit
"on the heart, mind, knowledge"

By doing saṃyama on the heart, you get knowledge of the mind.

III.35 सत्त्व पुरुषयोरत्यन्तासङ्कीर्णयोः प्रत्ययाविशेषो भोगः परार्थत्वात् स्वार्थसंयमात् पुरुष ज्ञानम्

sattva puruṣayoḥ atyanta asaṅkīrṇayoḥ pratyaya aviśeṣaḥ bhogaḥ para
    arthatvāt sva artha saṃyamāt puruṣa jñānam
"buddhi, puruṣa, totally, distinct, idea, not distinct, experience, another,
    purpose, own, purpose, from saṃyama, puruṣa, knowledge"

Patañjali says that buddhi and puruṣa, while they are totally distinct, are experienced as being the same. However, he also says that the buddhi only operates for another and not for it's own purpose. The 'other' here is puruṣa. By doing saṃyama on puruṣa with the idea of puruṣa being different from buddhi you get knowledge of puruṣa.

The philosophy is that an entity cannot directly perceive anything that is subtler than itself, and therefore buddhi can't directly perceive puruṣa by meditating on it because puruṣa is more subtle than buddhi. When rajas, and tamas are removed from buddhi, buddhi resembles puruṣa but is obviously not puruṣa. This is the knowledge that he's talking about in this sūtra. The buddhi gets imperfect knowledge of puruṣa from this, and while it's imperfect, it's a step in the right direction of knowing the difference between the two. Remember that you want to know the difference between them to attain mokṣa.

When the buddhi knows the difference it disconnects from puruṣa, and the puruṣa being totally alone, is only conscious of itself, and thus in kaivalyam. This is the idea of the puruṣa abiding in its own form forever that Patañjali discusses in I.3.

III.36 ततः प्रातिभ श्रावण वेदनादर्शास्वाद वार्ता जायन्ते

tataḥ prātibha śrāvaṇa vedana ādarśa āsvāda vārtāḥ jāyante
"from this, intuition, hearing, touch, seeing, taste, smell, are born"

Once you have the knowledge of puruṣa, as described in the previous sūtra, you get super-normal intuition, hearing, touch, sight, taste, smell, divine hearing, divine touch, etc. Vyāsa and Hariharānanda both say that you get these automatically.

III.37 ते समाधावुपसर्गा व्युत्थाने सिद्धयः

te samādhau upasargāḥ vyutthāne siddhayaḥ
"they, in samādhi, an obstacle, outgoing, powers"

Here Patañjali says that the powers (siddhis) are accomplishments to an outgoing mind, but are an impediment to samādhi. So you should ignore them. If you aren't interested in attaining mokṣa, and want to live in the world, they are accomplishments, but to yogīs, who are interested in attaining mokṣa, they are an obstacle to getting samādhi and therefore attaining mokṣa. This is because they tend to bring you back to the world.

It's unclear which siddhis Patañjali is talking about, and why he put this sūtra in the middle of the list of siddhis.

The siddhis, while they should, and would, be ignored by a serious yogī, can be looked upon as an indication that the yogī is making progress. If you get one you know you are making progress. If you later get another one you know that you are still making progress – but you will still ignore them as you know they are prakṛti, not the real you (puruṣa), and are therefore useless and uninteresting.

Patañjali may have also listed some of them in the text so that you will know you're not going crazy if you get them.

III.38 बन्ध कारण शैथिल्यात् प्रचार सम्वेदनाच् चित्तस्य पर शरीरावेशः

bandha kāraṇa śaithilyāt pracāra samvedanāt ca cittasya para śarīra
   āveśaḥ

"bound, cause, from relaxation, passageway, from knowledge, and, of
   the mind, other, body, entering into"

In this sūtra, Patañjali says you start to understand that you are not the body, and by knowledge of the mind, the you can enter into the body of someone else. Hariharānanda says that the bondage is caused by the idea that the yogī is the body (the kleśa of asmitā), and that by meditation the bondage is loosened or relaxed as the yogī comes to know that the yogī is not the body. Also, by meditation, the workings of the mind are understood and the yogī can then break free of the body and enter the body of another. Bryant says that this can be done, without the knowledge or permission of the newly entered body.

III.39 उदान जयाज्जल पङ्क कण्टकादिष्वसङ्ग उत्क्रान्तिश्च

udāna jayāt jala paṅka kaṇṭaka ādiṣu asaṅgaḥ utkrāntiḥ ca

"udāna, from mastery, water, mud, thorns, etc., non-contact, levitation, and"

When you master udāna you can't be immersed in water, mud, etc., can't be entangled in thorns, and you can levitate. Vyāsa says that this mastery allows you to leave your body (to die) at will. Udāna is one of the five prāṇas (life forces), which are listed below.

- prāṇa – inward moving prāṇa
- apāna – downward moving prāṇa
- samāna – digestive prāṇa
- udāna – upward moving prāṇa (to the head)
- vyāna – all over the body prāṇa

These prāṇas are well known and are just listed above for reference. There are also sub-prāṇas, but these are the five main ones.

III.40 समान जयाज्ज्वलनम्

samāna jayāt jvalanam

"samāna, from mastery, radiance"

When you master samāna (another of the prāṇas), you get radiance. The radiance is surrounding the body according to the commentators. According to Bryant, Vijñānabhikṣu says that this also gives you the ability to self combust, or burn yourself up using just prāṇa. Since samāna is the digestive fire this makes sense.

According to the Śiva Mahāpurāṇa, Satī, Lord Śiva's first wife, burned herself up, just using her own prāṇa, during a sacrifice being performed by her father, Dakṣa, after Dakṣa insulted Śiva. This apparently was where the practice of satī started. The practice of satī, which I've heard is now banned and not done anymore, was when a wife would throw herself on her husband's funeral pyre and burn up with her dead husband. Just to have a happy ending here, Satī was reincarnated as Pārvatī, who did tapas (austerities) for 4000 years so that Śiva would notice her and marry her again, which he did.

III.41 श्रोत्राकाशयोः सम्बन्ध संयमादिव्यं श्रोत्रम्

śrotra ākāśayoḥ sambandha saṃyamāt divyaṃ śrotram
"hearing, space/ether, relationship, from saṃyama, divine, hearing"

Here Patañjali says that by doing saṃyama on the relationship between hearing and ether, you get divine hearing. Since ākāśa (ether) pervades everything, the ear is also pervaded by ākāśa. Sound also travels through the ākāśa. When you meditate on the relationship between these two things you get the ability to hear anything anywhere. Bryant says that this applies to the other senses too.

III.42 कायाकाशयोः सम्बन्ध संयमाल्लघु तूल समापत्तेश्चाकाश गमनम्

kāya ākāśayoḥ sambandha saṃyamāt laghu tūla samāpatteḥ ca ākāśa
    gamanam
"body, ether, relationship, from saṃyama, light/not-heavy, cotton,
    samādhi, and, ether, motion"

Patañjali says that by doing saṃyama on the relationship between the body and ether, and doing samādhi on cotton, you can fly. Since the body, and all gross matter, are modifications (or derivatives of) ether, and since the yogī has control over these modifications, the yogī can make his atoms light, and therefore fly.

The first gross matter is ether or space which has the attribute of sound. The next form of gross matter is wind, which has the attribute of touch. It also contains ether. Ether and wind evolve into fire, which has the attribute of form. Fire contains both ether and wind. Next is water with the attribute of taste. It contains the previous three. Last is earth with the attribute of smell. And it contains all the previous four.

It's interesting to note that while the Sāṃkhya Kārikā, which is the document describing the metaphysics underpinning Patañjali's sūtras, mentions that gross matter (mahā bhūtas) comes out of subtle matter (tanmātras), and that there are five types of gross matter, it doesn't list them. It's unclear where the definition of the five types of gross matter come from. Perhaps it was a 'known' thing and not worth listing because everyone already knew it.

III.43 बहिरकल्पिता वृत्तिर्महा विदेहा ततः प्रकाशावरण क्षयः

bahiḥ akalpitā vṛttiḥ mahā videhā tataḥ prakāśa āvaraṇa kṣayaḥ

"external, real, state, great, bodiless, therefore, light, covering, destruction"

When the mind can be disconnected from the body and moved outside of the body, you get destruction of the covering over the buddhi. Vyāsa says that when you think the mind is outside the body, it's called akalpitā, or unimagined/real. When the mind is outside of the body, it's called mahā videhā, and when you move your mind outside the body, the mind can go into other bodies (see III.19 and III.20).

The point of this sūtra is that when you can move the mind out of the body it helps you lose the concept of "I am the body." This helps to get rid of the kleśas, especially asmitā. Remember from II.1 – II.11 that we need to get rid of the kleśas since they are obstacles to samādhi and mokṣa.

III.44 स्थूल स्वरूप सूक्ष्मान्वयार्थवत्त्व संयमाद्भूत जयः

sthūla sva rūpa sūkṣma anvaya arthavattva saṃyamāt bhūta jayaḥ

"gross, own, nature, subtle, constitution, purpose, from saṃyama, gross matter, mastery"

Here Patañjali is adding another siddhi about modifying matter. He says that by doing saṃyama on the gross nature, essential nature, subtle nature, and purpose, of gross matter, you get mastery over it. This ties in with previous thoughts on matter where the yogī can manipulate gross matter.

Gross nature is things like sound, earth, form, etc. Essential nature is the attributes of gross nature such as earth has hardness, water has liquidity, fire has heat, wind has mobility, ether has all pervasiveness. Note that this is different from the tanmātras which are subtle nature. Those are sound, touch, form, taste, and smell. Purpose is the experience it gives for enjoyment or liberation.

Since the mahā bhūtas come from the tanmātras, and the tanmātras come from ahaṃkāra, which comes from the buddhi, the yogī, by manipulating the specific qualities of objects can change them. This is mastery over them.

Note, as I said before, just because a yogī can do it, doesn't mean that they will. This applies to all manipulation of matter, and is because the universe is set up in a logical way and modifying it is dangerous. And since manipulation of matter doesn't give knowledge of puruṣa, it's uninteresting.

III.45 ततोऽणिमादिप्रादुर्भावः काय सम्पत्तद्धर्मानभिघातश्च

tataḥ aṇimā ādi prādur bhavaḥ kāya sampad tad dharma anabhighātaḥ ca
"Then, to become very small, etc., to manifest, state, body, perfection,
   their, nature, non-resistance, and"

Here Patañjali continues from the previous sūtra. He says, since the yogī gets mastery over gross matter as described III.44, the state of the body becomes perfect, there is no resistance from gross matter to the body, and you get eight other powers which, according to Vyāsa, are:

- aṇimā – ability to become very small
- laghimā – ability to be become very light and able to fly
- mahimā – ability to become large and heavy
- prāpti – ability to reach anything desired no matter how far away
- prakāmya – irresistible will (can go through solid rock, unable to be immersed in water, etc.)
- vaśitva – ability to control the elements and their qualities, and control other beings
- īśitṛtva – ability to control outward appearance, disappearance, and rearrangement of elements
- yatrakāmāvasāyitva – ability to manipulate the elements

Vyāsa goes on to discuss the non-resistance to the characteristics/nature of the body at this time. He says that the yogī can move through stone, water can't make it wet, fire can't burn them, wind doesn't affect them, and they can disappear in ākāśa (space).

III.46 रूप लावण्य बल वज्र संहननत्वानि काय सम्पत्

rūpa lāvaṇya bala vajra saṃhananatvāni kāya sampat
"form, beauty, strength, hard, texture, body, perfection"

Patañjali finishes the previous sūtra here, saying that perfection of the body is when the form of the body is beautiful, strong, and has a very hard texture.

III.47 ग्रहण स्व रूपास्मितान्वयार्थवत्त्व संयमादिन्द्रिय जयः

grahaṇa sva rūpa asmitā anvaya arthavattva saṃyamāt indriya jayaḥ
"process of knowledge, own, form, ego, connected with, serving a purpose, from saṃyama, senses, mastery"

In this sūtra Patañjali says that doing saṃyama on the process of knowing, on the form of the senses, on the ego, on the inter-connectedness and purpose of the senses, you get mastery over the senses. Here he's discussing the various aspects of the senses on the Sāṃkhya devolution tree as follows:

- process of knowledge – this is the gross sense organs themselves, which are derivatives of the tanmātras.
- essence – this is the senses as derivatives of the tanmātras (sight, sound, etc.)
- ego – this is the senses as derivatives of ahaṃkāra
- inter-connectedness/constitution/makeup – this is the senses as sattvic derivatives of buddhi
- purpose – this is the most subtle aspect of the senses

Vyāsa says that when you do saṃyama on these aspects in the order presented, you master the senses.

III.48 ततो मनो जविल्वं विकरण भाव: प्रधान जयश्च

tataḥ manaḥ javitvaṃ vikaraṇa bhāvaḥ pradhāna jayaḥ ca
"from that, mind, quickness, without a sense organ, state, primordial
   prakṛti, mastery, and"

Here Patañjali says that, from III.47, the body becomes as quick as the
mind, able to have the senses function without a sense organ, and gets
mastery over primordial prakṛti (pradhāna) and all its devolutes. At this point
the yogī has mastery and control over all prakṛti, but remember that the yogī
is not interested in manipulating prakṛti because he's only interested in
attaining mokṣa, and according to Patañjali, there's no prakṛti in mokṣa.

Section Summary

In this section Patañjali lists a bunch of siddhis/super-normal powers
that you can get from samādhi. While they seem fantastic, there are no texts
that say they don't exist. They can be used as signposts to know that you are
still making progress. However, in III.37 Patañjali says they are impediments
to samādhi.

III.49 – III.55 More on Attaining Mokṣa

At this point, Patañjali switches the focus again back to mokṣa. He spends the rest of the chapter on giving more information on how to attain mokṣa, which after all, is the point of the whole book.

III.49 सत्त्व पुरुषान्यता ख्याति मात्रस्य सर्व भावाधिष्ठातृत्वं सर्व ज्ञातृत्वं च

sattva puruṣa anyatā khyāti mātrasya sarva bhāva adhiṣṭhātṛtvaṃ sarva
    jñātṛtvaṃ ca
"buddhi, puruṣa, difference, knowledge, only, all, state, authority/
    supremacy, all, knowing, and"

Here Patañjali says that only if you have the knowledge of the difference between buddhi and puruṣa, i.e. viveka khyātiḥ, do you get omniscience and omnipotence (supremacy over all states of prakṛti).

Patañjali is using the word 'sattva' instead of buddhi because, since the buddhi is almost pure sattva, sattva is sometimes used as a synonym for buddhi. Since the buddhi is involved, this is still samprajñāta samādhi (I.17 and I.41 – I.46). And since everything manifest comes from prakṛti, you have mastery over all matter.

III.50 तद्वैराग्यादपि दोष बीज क्षये कैवल्यम्

tad vairāgyāt api doṣa bīja kṣaye kaivalyam
"that, from non-attachment, even, imperfection, seed, on destruction,
    liberation"

Patañjali says that when you aren't attached to even 'that' (omnipotence and omniscience), and you destroy the seeds of imperfection (the kleśas), you get liberation. Due to non-attachment, you actually get rid of the kleśas (II.1 – II.11), and since you know the difference between puruṣa and buddhi (from the previous sūtra), you find the buddhi uninteresting, and the mind shuts off and disconnects from puruṣa, which is mokṣa as discussed in I.47 – I.51. At this point you are in asamprajñāta samādhi where the puruṣa is only conscious of itself since it has no connection to prakṛti anymore, and there's nothing else to be conscious of.

III.51 स्थान्युपनिमन्त्रणे सङ्ग स्मयाकरणं पुनरनिष्ट प्रसङ्गात्

sthāni upa nimantraṇe saṅga smaya akaraṇam punar aniṣṭa prasaṅgāt
"celestial beings, with, invitation, attachment, pride, without cause,
    again, undesirable, from attachment"

In this sūtra Patañjali says that you should not have pride in, or attachment to, an invitation by celestial beings to go to the celestial realms, because you may get an undesirable attachment. Patañjali doesn't mention how the celestial beings will invite you. He's discussing another possible distraction and way to fall from the yogic path. The celestial beings are also prakṛti and you don't want to have any attachment with prakṛti. I've heard that some of the celestial beings will try to keep you involved in the pleasures of prakṛti. The problem with accepting the invitation of the celestial beings is that even though you may get to the celestial realms and have great pleasure, sooner or later you will have to be reborn and return to this world where everything is painful/non-satisfying.

III.52 क्षण तत्क्रमयो: संयमाद्विवेकजं ज्ञानम्

kṣaṇa tat kramayoḥ saṃyamāt viveka jaṃ jñānam

"moment, that, sequence, from saṃyama, discrimination, born, knowledge"

Here Patañjali gives another way to get viveka khyātiḥ (discriminative wisdom). Vyāsa says that by doing saṃyama on the present moment you get knowledge of the future changing into the present, and the present changing into the past. This is discrimination born from knowledge. To discuss this we need to know a bit about some Saṃskṛtam words.

First, an 'anu' is the smallest manifestation of prakṛti possible that is still a mahā bhūta (ether, air, fire, water, and earth). An anu doesn't have any parts and cannot be divided. The definition of an anu keeps changing as science gets more knowledgeable in the area of subatomic particles. At one time it could have been equated to an atom, but now that we know about quarks, muons, etc., it's not that anymore.

'Moment' in this sūtra is the period that it takes for an anu to have a detectable change. Time, according to Vyāsa, is a sequence of these moments. In I.40 Patañjali said that the yogī's mastery extends from the smallest particle (anu) to the entire universe, and in III.49 an advanced yogī, is omniscient and omnipotent. Therefore, from III.49, the yogi can detect a change in an anu.

III.53 जाति लक्षण देशैरन्यतानवच्छेदात्तुल्ययोस्ततः प्रतिपत्तिः

jāti lakṣaṇa deśaiḥ anyatā anavacchedāt tulyayoḥ tataḥ pratipattiḥ

"species, characteristic, place, difference, without distinction, two similar things, then, ascertainment"

Patañjali says, after the previous sūtra, the yogī can tell the difference between two things that are the same (without distinction), regardless of the species, characteristics, or place. Vyāsa has an interesting discussion of this. He says that if you have two objects that are exactly the same, while normal people can't tell the difference, the yogī can because they can see the sequence (from the previous sūtra) that brought both objects to their current place. He even says that if you have two identical objects, one in front and one in back, and switch them around while the yogī is not looking, the yogī will know that they've been switched because their sequences will show this.

III.54 तारकं सर्व विषयं सर्वथा विषयमक्रमं चेति विवेकजं ज्ञानम्

tārakaṃ sarva viṣayam sarvathā viṣayam akramam ca iti viveka jaṃ jñānam

"intuition, all, objects, in all ways, objects, without sequence/simultane-
ously, and, this, discrimination, born, knowledge"

In III.52 Patañjali said that, through intuition, you can know the sequence from a single moment, and in III.53 he said that you can always tell the difference between any two objects by their sequences. Here Patañjali continues from the previous sūtra again, saying that knowledge born of discrimination, from comprehension of all objects completely (in all ways and all times), simultaneously, is intuition and can't be acquired from study. Also, because of the knowledge of the sequences you can see the past, present, and future. Vyāsa says that this knowledge leads to liberation (mokṣa).

III.55 सत्त्व पुरुषयोः शुद्धि साम्ये कैवल्यम्

sattva puruṣayoḥ śuddhi sāmye kaivalyam
"buddhi, puruṣa, pure, the same, liberation"

This is the final sūtra of the third chapter. Here Patañjali says that when the purity of the buddhi is the same as the puruṣa, you attain liberation/mokṣa. At this point in your sādhana, you will have removed all the rajas and tamas from your buddhi. Because of this, Patañjali uses the word sattva for buddhi. All the kleśas are gone, and the buddhi knows the difference between itself and puruṣa. Then the buddhi disconnects from puruṣa and dissolves/disappears, thus attaining mokṣa. Now that the puruṣa is disconnected from prakṛti, the only thing that it can be conscious of is itself (since consciousness is eternal), and it exists all alone, in a joyful state of bliss forever. This is what Patañjali was talking about in I.3 where he said that mokṣa is when the puruṣa abides in its own form forever.

Section Summary

In this section Patañjali says that viveka khyātiḥ (discriminative wisdom) is the only way to attain mokṣa. He then says that from para vairāgya (highest non-attachment) you get omniscience. He also says not to get pride from, or accept, the invitations from celestial beings since this won't help you attain mokṣa. He then discusses another way to get viveka khyātiḥ, by meditating on the sequences of matter. He finishes up saying that when your buddhi is as pure as your puruṣa, you attain mokṣa.

Chapter Summary

In this chapter Patañjali starts by discussing the last three limbs of Aṣṭāṅga Yoga: dhāraṇā (concentration), dhyāna (meditation), and samādhi (the tool you use in meditation to get the knowledge you need to attain mokṣa. He spends most of the rest of the chapter discussing the super-normal powers you get from samādhi. He does say in sūtra 37 that the super-normal powers are an obstacle to samādhi. He finishes up the chapter with some thoughts on attaining mokṣa, finishing up with the statement that when your buddhi is as pure as your puruṣa, you attain liberation/mokṣa.

Kaivalya Pāda

IV.1 – IV.6 Miscellaneous

This chapter has a number of different sections: more on the siddhis from the previous chapter, saṃskāras and karma and rebirth, properties of prakṛti and their association with the mind, comments on acquisition of knowledge, and finally more on attaining mokṣa. It appears that Patañjali had published the first three chapters, and later wrote the fourth to include things that he forgot and to add more information and clarification on a number of topics, including metaphysics, samādhi, and mokṣa. Unfortunately, in the last section of this chapter he uses different terminology than he used in the first three chapters. I'll try to note these and explain them when we get there.

IV.1 जन्मौषधि मन्त्र तपः समाधिजाः सिद्धयः

janma oṣadhi mantra tapaḥ samādhi jāḥ siddhayah
"birth, herbs, sacred chants, austerity, samādhi, caused by, powers"

Patañjali starts this chapter with a sūtra discussing different ways that you can get the siddhis detailed in the previous chapter. He says that by being born with them, herbs (psychedelic drugs), chanting and incantations, austerities, and samādhi, you can get the siddhis (super-normal powers).

You might get siddhis if you were previously a celestial, a videhā (bodiless one), or prakṛti-laya (enmeshed in prakṛti) (I.19), and now born as a human. The use of herbs/drugs can give them to you, but because you don't control them this way they aren't very useful for yoga. Mantras and incantations were used by Vedic people to affect material reality, and this use also is not very useful for yogīs since yogīs are not interested in manipulating material reality. It's not the puruṣa. Austerity was used in many stories as ways to get siddhis from the gods, but they were used to get powers for personal gain and not used for attaining mokṣa.

However, you will remember that Patañjali also said in III.37 that siddhis are an impediment to samādhi. So a yogī that is interested in getting into samādhi in order to attain mokṣa should ignore them. They may be useful to know that you are making progress in your sādhana, but after you note that, you should just go and meditate some more.

IV.2 जात्यन्तर परिणामः प्रकृत्यापूरात्

jāti antara pariṇāmaḥ prakṛti āpūrāt

"species, inside, transformation, prakṛti, filling in"

In this sūtra Patañjali is adding to his discussion from II.12 – II.14 about karma. Here he says that when you get reborn, whatever the species, the form is 'filled in' by prakṛti. You can look at the 'filling in' like a mold for whatever body you get, and prakṛti is poured into it, filling it up, and taking the form, mind, and organs, of the new body. The message here is that if you change species only the saṃskāras that pertain to that species are available, so if you change from a human to a dog, you become totally a dog, not a human trapped in a dog form. All of your thinking will be correct for a dog.

IV.3 निमित्तमप्रयोजकं प्रकृतीनां वरण भेदस्तु ततः क्षेत्रिक वत्

nimittam aprayojakaṃ prakritīnāṃ varaṇa bhedaḥ tu tataḥ kṣetrika vat

"cause, not leading to, natural state, choosing, breaking/splitting, obstacle, but, farmer, like"

Here Patañjali is discussing how things change in prakṛti. The idea is that the guṇas are always changing, but they can only change in certain ways. Actions (the cause) do not directly make (lead to) the change, but they remove the barrier to change, and nature (prakṛti) changes its state based on its own rules.

The example Patañjali gives is a farmer that has a dike holding water for their fields. If the farmer wants to water the field, the farmer doesn't push the water from the pond to the field. Instead the farmer removes the barrier between the pond that the field and the water flows on its own. Another facet to this is that the water held back by the dike or obstacle moves only in the direction that is possible when the barrier is removed. If the farmer removes the barrier to the north field, the water goes to the north field and not the south field. Removing the obstacle to change allows the change to happen and affects the possible changes but does not actually make the change. Removing the barrier doesn't cause the water to flow into the field. Flowing is the nature of water, but the removal of the barrier allows it to flow.

Another example that is more relevant to a yogī is the following. Patañjali says that you need to meditate to get viveka khyātiḥ (discriminative wisdom) in order to attain mokṣa. However, if your body hurts when sitting to meditate, it's difficult to make progress. The practice of āsana is intended to give you a strong, healthy, flexible, body so that you can meditate. So āsana removes the pain that keeps you from meditating, but it doesn't cause you to meditate, or cause you to attain mokṣa. Since your body and citta (mind) are both prakṛti, this example applies here.

IV.4 निर्माण चित्तान्यस्मिता मात्रात्

nirmāṇa cittāni asmitā mātrāt
"making, minds, ego, only"

This, and the next two sūtras discuss another miscellaneous topic: created minds. Patañjali says that yogīs can create minds, and those minds are created from ego only. However, he doesn't say why a yogī would want to do this. All the commentators agree that this is a real thing. It appears in various texts, not just Patañjali. However, as usual, Patañjali doesn't give any information on how to do this, just like he didn't give any explicit āsanas to do, or which prāṇāyāma practices to do.

Cittāni is plural, so Patañjali is saying that more than one could be created. The commentators all say that a body is created for each mind. The questions of whether each created body has it's own mind or there is only the yogī's mind in each one, and how karma affects them are answered in the next couple of sūtras.

IV.5 प्रवृत्ति भेदे प्रयोजकं चित्तमेकमनेकेषाम्

pravṛtti bhede prayojakaṃ cittam ekam anekeṣām
"activities, different, controller, mind, one, not one"

Though the activities of the different minds vary, the one mind that created them is the controller of the many. Here Patañjali says that even though the created minds, and bodies, are doing different things, they are controlled by the yogī that created them. Vācaspati Miśra says the yogī can destroy them all at will.

Hariharānanda discusses how one mind can control the others since they are separated. He says that the answer lies in IV.10 where Patañjali says that the yogī's mind is all pervasive, i.e. it's everywhere. Due to this, the controller mind can easily contact and control the others since it's already pervading them. Vyāsa says that the yogī creates one mind and makes it the controller of the other minds. However, it's not clear if Vyāsa means that the yogī's mind is the controller or if the yogī creates a mind just to control the others. However, Vijñānabhikṣu, according to Bryant, says that the controller mind is the yogī's mind.

IV.6 तत्र ध्यान जमनाशयम्

tatra dhyāna jam anāśayam
"of these, meditation, born, without a seat/place/resting-place"

Here, Patañjali says that of the created minds, only the ones born (created) by meditation are without karma. All the commentators add 'for karma' to seat/place/resting-place. So the yogī's mind is the only one that is subject to karma and rebirth for those created minds.

Vyāsa says that a mind created by meditation doesn't have karma because the yogī who has created it has removed their kleśas (by making them like roasted seeds and therefore dormant) by that point, and kleśas cause karma. The minds created by the other methods – birth, drugs, incantations, and austerities (see IV.1), are subject to karma because they have a karmāśaya because the person who created them has one.

These few sūtras are confusing because they don't explain why a yogī would want to create other minds. It could be that Patañjali just wanted to add some more siddhis.

<u>Section Summary</u>

In this section Patañjali first says that there are five ways to get the powers/siddhis: birth, herbs, sacred chants, austerity, and samādhi. Getting them from samādhi is the only way used by yogīs. Then he has a sūtra saying that when you get born into a different species than the last birth, prakṛti 'fills in' the new body with only saṃskāras appropriate for that species. The third sūtra explains that actions don't cause changes in material nature. All an action can do is to remove the obstacle to change due to the rules of prakṛti. Then he gives information on yogīs creating minds and bodies. He doesn't say how or why you would do this, though.

IV.7 – IV.11 Saṃskāras, Vāsanās, Karma, and Rebirth

If you remember, Patañjali only spent three sūtras discussing saṃskāras, karma, and rebirth (II.12 – II.14). Here he adds some more information on this topic. In IV.7 he introduces a new term, vāsanā, which I'll discuss below. In this section he discusses the various types of karma, and how your saṃskāras handle differing species in the various births during your sādhana.

IV.7 कर्माशुक्लाकृष्णं योगिनस्त्रिविधमितरेषाम्

karma aśukla akṛṣṇaṃ yoginaḥ tri vidham itareṣām

"action, not white, not black, yogī, three, kinds, the other people"

In this sūtra Patañjali says that the actions of a yogī are are neither black nor white. This is because yogīs do action that doesn't count as action. Then he says that the actions of others (non-yogīs) are of three kinds: black actions are adharmic (bad), white are dharmic (good), and the third kind are both black and white. The last type just mentioned is various shades of gray, depending where on the spectrum between dharma (good) and adharma (bad) the action is. This one is where many of the actions of most people are: they contain both dharmic and adharmic components. The important thing here is that yogīs actions don't count as actions, and therefore aren't karma, while the actions of non-yogīs are karma, the results of which need to experienced.

In the Bhagavad Gītā, in IV.20, Kṛṣṇa says that a yogī who does action without wanting the results of the action does not do any action. That is, your intent when doing an action determines whether it is an action and will produce a karmic fruit or not. In IV.23 he says that actions by someone who has no attachments to prakṛti and is liberated, whose mind is steady in the knowledge of action, and only does action as a sacrifice to him, are completely dissolved. These two ślokas (sentences) are the essence of Kṛṣṇa's definition of karma yoga, or the yoga of action.

One of my students objected to black being bad and white being good, thinking that this was racist. To remove any thoughts that there is a fundamental racism based on skin color, note that Kṛṣṇa's name means black, and he was black/dark skinned.

IV.8 ततस्तद्विपाकानुगुणानामेवाभिव्यक्तिर्वासनानाम्

tataḥ tad vipāka anuguṇānām eva abhivyaktiḥ vāsanānām
"from those, their, ripening, having similar qualities, exactly, upon manifestation, mental impression"

Here Patañjali says that, from the four types of karma mentioned in the
previous sūtra, when the fruit/result of the action 'ripen' by manifesting in
rebirth, you get vāsanās/saṃskāra appropriate for that birth. Vāsanās are
basically saṃskāras. So what he's saying here is that when you get born, only
the vāsanas that make sense for that species you are born in become
available/ripen/fructify. So if you are a human you get vāsanās appropriate
for a human. If you're born as a dog you get vāsanās appropriate for a dog.
For example, in the first case you might get the vāsanā of speech, whereas in
the second case you would get the vāsanā of barking. Remember, that you
are continually adding saṃskāras to your store of saṃskāras all throughout
your various lives in the various species that you have been born in.

Patañjali uses the term vāsanā instead of saṃskāra in this sūtra. Bryant
says that the commentators don't always distinguish between the two words.

IV.9 जाति देश काल व्यवहितानामप्यानन्तर्यं स्मृति संस्कारयोरेक रूपत्वात्

jāti deśa kāla vyavahitānām api ānantaryaṃ smṛti saṃskarayoḥ eka rū-
patvāt
"species, place, time, separated by, even, not uninterrupted, memory,
saṃskāra, one, form"

In this sūtra Patañjali continues discussing karma and rebirth. He says
that even though interrupted by species, place, and time, memories and
saṃskāras have the same single form. What he's saying is that when you are
reborn, all the saṃskāras and memories from the last time you had that
species appear no matter how many lifetimes ago they were created, whether

in the previous life or 1,000 lifetimes ago. So if you are born as a cat, the samskāras and memories from the last time you were cat, such as liking to hunt and eat mice, appear the next time you are born as a cat, regardless of how long ago and how many different species you were born as between the two cat births.

To handle/avoid the question of about how species-specific samskāras are created for the first time, Indic philosophers just say that the process was beginningless (see the next sūtra).

IV.10 तासामनादित्वं चाशिषो नित्यत्वात्

tāsām anāditvaṃ ca āśiṣaḥ nityatvāt
"their, having no beginning, and, desire to live, eternal"

This adds on to the previous sūtra. Patañjali says that samskāras have no beginning because the desire for life is eternal. Here he's using 'their' to mean the samskāras from the previous sūtra.

IV.11 हेतु फलाश्रयालम्बनैः संगृहितत्वादेषामभावे तदभावः

hetu phala āśraya alambanaiḥ saṅgrhitatvāt eṣām abhāve tad abhāvaḥ
"cause, fruit, basis, support, because of being held together, of these,
    non-existence, those, existence"

In this last of the sūtras on karma and rebirth, Patañjali says that because samskāras are held together (they are made up of) cause, fruit, basis, and support, and therefore samskāras don't exist when those four things don't exist.

- The cause is avidyā (ignorance)
- The fruit is the result of the action (you do the action to get the fruit)
- The basis is a mind that doesn't have discriminative wisdom (viveka khyātiḥ)
- The support is the object that causes the samskāra or vāsanā to be activated

Remember that you have to get rid of (make them dormant) all of your saṃskāras in order to attain mokṣa as described in I.50 and I.51. You also have to get rid of the kleśas (II.2 – II.11). In II.15 – II.28 Patañjali discusses how to get discriminative wisdom (viveka khyātiḥ) so you get mokṣa. Remember that this is a many-lifetime process and you slowly get rid of your kleśas over many lifetimes.

To explain the fruit and support, I will use the example of my favorite description of the kleśa rāga (desire and attachment). If I have desire (rāga) for cookies, when I see cookies, my saṃskāra for cookies causes a vṛtti in my mind to get the cookies. Therefore, the cookies are the support/object that activates my cookie saṃskāra, and the fruit of my action is enjoying the cookies. When I get rid of my desire (rāga) for cookies, I may still like and enjoy them, I just won't desire them; if they're available I will eat them, but if they're not I won't be unhappy.

When you get rid of avidyā, all the rest of the kleśas are gone since avidyā is the field for the other kleśas to grow: they exist in avidyā. If you remember, discriminative wisdom (viveka khyātiḥ) is the knowledge of the difference between puruṣa and prakṛti; not the intellectual knowledge but the knowledge acquired through samādhi. This is the ṛtambharā (truth bearing wisdom) described in I.48.

Section Summary

In this section Patañjali gives more information about karma than he gave in II.12 – II.14, discussing how the actions (karma) of yogīs (not black or white) are different from non-yogīs (black, white, or both black and white). He then says that, since actions (karma) done in previous lives affect the species you are born with (II.13), you get the saṃskāras/vāsanās from previous lives that are appropriate to the current life. He also says that you get the appropriate saṃskāras and vāsanās for the species of your current life regardless of how many lives you have experienced since the last time you were born in that species.

IV.12 – IV.22 Metaphysics

In this section Patañjali discusses metaphysics in more detail than earlier in the text. He talks about what's real and thoughts connecting puruṣa and prakṛti. I think that since Patañjali didn't discuss metaphysics much at all in the previous chapters, and so he's doing it here to clarify what he said earlier. Bryant suggests that the reason for this section is to refute the Buddhists, who were his major opponents at the time; since their metaphysics are different he needed to define his own.

IV.12 अतीतानागतं स्वरुपतोऽस्त्यध्वभेदाद्धर्माणाम्

atīta anāgatam svarūpataḥ asti adhva bhedāt dharmāṇām

"past, future, in reality, exist, time, difference, characteristic"

In this sūtra Patañjali says that the past and the future, and therefore prakṛti, always exist due to the difference in time when the characteristics of prakṛti, in the past and future, appear. According to Vyāsa, the future is the unmanifest result of the present, and the past is the unmanifest expression of things that were experienced in the present, and the present is the manifest expression what was the future and what will be the past. For example, if you have a pot in the present, it had the characteristics of clay in the past, and also has the characteristics of shards in the future. To use the movie metaphor again, it's like the individual frames in the film; while you can only see the current frame, the past and future frames still exist.

This idea is supported by the Sāṃkhya doctrine of satkāryavāda which says that nothing is ever created (or destroyed for that matter); things just change their characteristics, like clay which is changed into a pot, which changes into shards, which change into dust. None of these things are created, they are all just modifications of the characteristics of clay.

And since prakṛti is always changing, but puruṣa never changes, which Patañjali discusses in II.20, IV.17, and IV.18, this is how the past and future are aspects of prakṛti, and how it relates to this sūtra.

IV.13 ते व्यक्त सूक्ष्मा गुणात्मानः

te vyakta sūkṣmāḥ guṇa ātmānaḥ

"they, manifest, subtle, guṇas, nature of"

Patañjali continues from the previous sūtra, saying that the past, present, and future, are either manifest or subtle, and are of the nature of the three guṇas (sattva: peaceful/light, rajas: activity/heat, tamas: inactivity/dark). According to Sāṃkhya, everything other than puruṣa is made up of prakṛti and is described by the guṇas (see II.15 for a discussion of the guṇas).

According to Kṛṣṇa in the Bhagavad Gītā, II.28, beings are unmanifest (subtle) in the beginning, manifest in the middle, and in the end are unmanifest (subtle) again. In II.39 Patañjali said that when you master non-acceptance you get knowledge of previous and future births, so you can access the past and the future. In the previous sutra and this one, he's explaining why you can see the past and future; they are real and always exist.

IV.14 परिणामैकत्वाद्वस्तु तत्त्वम्

pariṇāma ekatvāt vastu tattvam

"transformation, oneness, object, real"

Here Patañjali is adding more to the idea of the reality of prakṛti by saying that because there are consistent rules (oneness) governing how prakṛti changes (transforms), it must be real. Due to the principle of satkāryavāda, transformations are defined, limited, bound by rules, and can be understood. For example, you can change milk into yogurt but not into steel.

Some of the commentators posit that, with this sūtra, Patañjali is contradicting the Buddhist 'idealists' that maintain that objects are not real. They assume that objects only 'exist' when they are thought of, but, because you can have cognition of an object in dreams without the existence of that object, they don't really exist at all. Vyāsa says that Buddhist 'idealists' give up the objective world on the strength of imaginative cognition, and they go on talking nonsense about it. He continues, asking how is it possible to have faith in them?

<u>The important thing to remember here is that Patañjali maintains that prakṛti, and therefore the buddhi, ahaṃkāra, subtle matter, and gross matter, are real.</u>

IV.15 वस्तु साम्ये चित्त भेदात्तयोर्विभक्तः पन्थाः

vastu sāmye citta bhedāt tayoḥ vibhaktaḥ panthāḥ
"object, common, mind, difference, their, different, path"

Patañjali says here that because multiple minds perceive a common object differently, there is a difference between the minds, due to the different paths that they have followed to get to where they are perceiving the object, i.e. their history. He says that if you have two minds perceiving the same object, each one is going to perceive it differently due to the two person's saṃskāras, and therefore there must be a difference between minds.

For example, one person may really like the taste of steak, while a Hindu will revere a cow. If both are viewing the same cow, they will have different perceptions of the same cow: tasty vs. reverence. Patañjali is saying that since the two minds have different perceptions of the same cow, objects are not created by minds since two minds can perceive the same cow, and also shows that minds are different. This is his argument that there is a multiplicity of minds and therefore puruṣas since there's one puruṣa for each mind (except the mind-created ones discussed earlier in this chapter).

IV.16 न चैक चित्त तन्त्रं वस्तु तदप्रमाणकं तदा किं स्यात्

na ca eka citta tantraṃ vastu tad apramāṇakaṃ tadā kiṃ syāt
"not, and, one, mind, dependent, object, that, not authoritative, then,
    what, it may be"

In this sūtra Patañjali says that an object is not dependent on one mind. He says, if a mind stops perceiving an object (is not authoritative), and the object still exists, then what is the cause of the object? This is a continuation from the last sūtra where he argued that there is a difference between minds and objects, and that there are multiple minds. Now he says that objects are not created by minds because if they were, what would happen if the creating mind stops perceiving it? He's also adding on to II.22 where Patañjali said that while prakṛti is 'destroyed' for a puruṣa that has attained mokṣa, it still exists for others.

Another way to look at this is to think about a corollary from the previous sūtra. If two minds are perceiving the same cow, what happens to the cow when one of the minds stops perceiving the cow? If objects are created by minds, and the cow was created by the mind that is not perceiving the cow anymore, what does the other mind perceive? Obviously the other mind continues to perceive the cow. Therefore, objects are real.

Vyāsa has an interesting comment. He asks if an object only exists by being perceived by a mind, and the perceiver only sees the front of the object, does the object have a back? He responds to the question, saying that it doesn't make sense to have a front and not a back, and therefore, objects are real and not dependent on being cognized by a mind.

IV.17 तदुपरागापेक्षित्वाच्चित्तस्य वस्तु ज्ञाताज्ञातम्

tad uparāga apekṣitvāt cittasya vastu jñāta ajñātam

"that, colored, dependent, of the mind, object, known, not known"

Patañjali here uses 'colored' to mean that the mind is aware of an object, thus 'coloring' the mind. The point he's trying to make is that because objects are sometimes known and sometimes not known by the mind, the mind changes.

The important thing here, according to Vyāsa, is that because objects are sometimes known and sometimes not known, this proves that the mind is changeable, and therefore made up of prakṛti. This is a fundamental assumption about prakṛti: it's always changing. This is part of Patañjali's discussion on metaphysics and is used, here, and in the next sūtra, to elaborate on the difference between the mind, which changes, and puruṣa, which doesn't change.

There is still the problem that the philosophy says that to be eternal, a thing cannot change: prakṛti is always changing but it's eternal. Patañjali never addresses this problem.

IV.18 सदा ज्ञाताश्चित्त वृत्तयस्तत्प्रभोः पुरुषस्यापरिणामित्वात्

sadā jñātāḥ citta vṛttayaḥ tat prabhoḥ puruṣasya apariṇāmitvāt
"always, known, mind, changing, its, master, puruṣa, unchanging"

This is a continuation of the previous sūtra, where Patañjali said that the mind changes, because it sometimes is aware of an object and sometimes not aware of that object. Here he says that the mind is always known to the puruṣa (its master), which doesn't change. Vyāsa says that if the puruṣa was changing then the changes of the mind would sometimes be known to the puruṣa, and sometimes not. Then he says because the mind is always known to the puruṣa, this proves that the puruṣa is unchangeable. Remember that it's assumed that to be eternal, a thing cannot change; if it changed, then it wouldn't be the same and is therefore not eternal.

This is an extension to II.20 where he said that the puruṣa sees, i.e. is conscious of the contents of the mind. The difference here is that Patañjali now says that the puruṣa is <u>always</u> aware of the mind (citta).

IV.19 न तत्स्वाभासं दृश्यत्वात्

na tat sva ābhāsaṃ dṛśyatvāt
"not, its, self, illuminating, because it's perceptible"

In this sūtra, and the next, Patañjali does this by giving some definitional information on perception, and then using that to show that there's a difference between puruṣa and prakṛti, and that they both exist.

Vācaspati Miśra, in his commentary on the next sūtra, discusses the difference between self illuminating and object illuminating. Self illuminating means that the entity can perceive itself and objects, while object illuminating means that the entity can only perceive objects. The commentators all say that puruṣa can perceive, or be conscious of, itself and objects, but the mind, which is prakṛti, can only perceive objects of prakṛti. This is an assumption of both Sāṃkhya and Patañjali. The important corollary to this is that, since the mind is perceivable, it can't be self illuminating, or perceive itself.

In this sūtra Patañjali says that it (mind) is not self illuminating because it can be perceived. To explain this, Hariharanada asks the question "Why isn't the mind a knower, since it 'knows' that it's happy, sad, etc.?". He responds with another question: "Who knows I'm the knower?". Hariharanada says the answer to that question is "I know I'm the knower." He then says that this proves that there is something that knows/perceives, that is different from the rest of the mind. He finishes up, saying that the act of knowing is perception, while that which perceives is pure consciousness. Since the only thing that is conscious is puruṣa, he says that this proves the difference between the puruṣa and the mind (prakṛti), and that they both exist. The mind appears to be conscious due to the conjunction with puruṣa, but it's not.

IV.20 एक समये चोभयानवधारणम्

eka samaye ca ubhaya an avadhāraṇam
"one, time, and, both, not, cognizable"

This sūtra continues from the previous one. Here Patañjali says that the mind cannot simultaneously be aware of both itself and another object at the same time.

Vyāsa says that this sūtra and the previous one are a refutation of the Buddhist notion of momentariness, where things only exist for a moment; during that moment, there is a change, and therefore it's a different thing. He says that to those who believe in momentariness, the doer, the action, and the result of the action are the same, and therefore all three things would be perceived simultaneously; in other words, the mind would have to be aware of itself and the object of action at the same time. Then he says that since this is not the case, based on this sūtra, the mind cannot be considered self luminous. The point of this argument is that if the mind is not self luminous, it's not conscious as noted in the previous sūtra, and therefore both puruṣa and prakṛti, are distinct and they both exist.

IV.21 चित्तान्तर दृश्ये बुद्धि बुद्धेरतिप्रसङ्गः स्मृति सङ्करश्च

citta antara dṛśye buddhi buddheḥ atiprasaṅgaḥ smṛti saṅkaraḥ ca
"mind, another, in being seen, buddhi, of buddhi, excessive attachment,
 memory, confusion, and"

Patañjali says that the mind of one person cannot see the mind of another person because being able to do that would cause an excessive attachment and confusion of memory. He's pointing out here that if one mind could see another's mind, then the other mind could also see the first mind, and the first mind would then see the second mind seeing the first mind, etc. This would cause an infinite regress and confusion of memories, just like when you put a penny on a mirror and put another mirror upside down on the penny. When you do this you see an infinite number of pennies.

This sūtra seems like a clarification of III.19 where Patañjali said that by doing saṃyama on another's thoughts you can get knowledge of them, and then in III.20 he said that you can't get the object in the other person's mind because only the thoughts about the object are there, and not the actual object. In this sūtra Patañjali is saying that you can get some knowledge of the other person's thoughts but can't actually see the other person's mind.

IV.22 चितेरप्रतिसङ्क्रमायास्तदाकारापत्तौ स्वबुद्धिसंवेदनम्

citeḥ apratisaṅkramāyāḥ tat ākāra āpattau sva buddhi saṃvedanam
"of consciousness, unchanging, that, form, pervading, own, buddhi,
 knowing"

This is the last sūtra on metaphysics. Patañjali says that while consciousness (puruṣa) is unchanging, it does pervade the form of its own buddhi, and is thus conscious (knows) of its buddhi. This explains how the puruṣa is conscious of the buddhi even though it never changes. Remember from IV.18 where Patañjali states that the puruṣa never changes: a requirement for being eternal.

Vyāsa says that the puruṣa is unchangeable. He goes on to say that it appears to follow the changing states of the buddhi, which makes the buddhi seem to be conscious, and this causes them to seem to be the same, which is asmitā (II.6).

This sūtra explains how the puruṣa is conscious of the buddhi. This is important because the buddhi needs to 'be conscious' in order to understand the difference between puruṣa and prakṛti in order to attain mokṣa. The buddhi uses the consciousness of the puruṣa to follow a yogic sādhana (path) to get this understanding. In II.15 – II.28 Patañjali discusses that the buddhi needs to get rid of its avidyā by getting viveka khyātiḥ (discriminative wisdom) to attain mokṣa. The buddhi starts in ignorance (avidyā), and by going through the levels of samprajñāta samādhi it gets the knowledge of the difference between puruṣa and prakṛti.

Section Summary

In this section Patañjali first shows that material objects (prakṛti) are real – in the past, present, and future, and because changes in objects are bound by consistent rules. He then shows that there are multiple minds because different people perceive the same object differently, and that objects are not created by minds, because objects continue to exist even after a mind stops perceiving them. He continues on, showing that the mind changes while the puruṣa doesn't. Then he shows that puruṣa and prakṛti both exist and they are different because the puruṣa can perceive the mind (prakṛti) but the mind cannot perceive the puruṣa. He finishes up the section discussing how the puruṣa is conscious of the mind.

In the next section Patañjali discusses the buddhi more, how it works towards attaining mokṣa, and concludes with some final thoughts on attaining mokṣa.

IV.23 – IV.34 Final thoughts on the Buddhi and Mokṣa

In this, the final section of the sūtras, Patañjali gives information about the buddhi and how it attains mokṣa. Some of what he says here repeats what he said in the first chapter, but there is new information, including some new terminology.

IV.23 द्रष्टृ दृश्योपरक्तं चित्तं सर्वार्थम्

draṣṭṛ dṛśya uparaktaṃ cittaṃ sarva artham
"seer, seen, color, the mind, all, objects"

Patañjali starts this section talking about Īśvara by saying that both the seer (puruṣa) and the seen (prakṛti) color the mind, and therefore the mind (citta) knows all objects. In other words, it's omniscient, but only after you get rid of all rajas and tamas in the mind (for more information on this point see IV.31 later in this section). This may seem to contradict I.25 where Patañjali said that the omniscience of Īśvara is unsurpassed. But here, Patañjali is saying that, while the mind is also omniscient, it's less omniscient than Īśvara. This seems bizarre unless we accept Bryant's suggestion that the mind is omniscient about prakṛti but not about puruṣa, and Īśvara is omniscient about both. Also, in Sāṃkhya 35, it says that the buddhi, ahaṃkāra, and manas (the three parts of the citta) comprehend all objects, also indicating that the citta is omniscient.

The mind is modified (colored) by the object it is thinking about, and because the mind also has a relationship with the puruṣa it's also modified by that. The modification by puruṣa is the appearance of consciousness only, because as you remember, the puruṣa doesn't actually 'do' anything; the mind appears to be conscious, but it's not, and only looks that way because of the relationship with the puruṣa.

IV.24 तदसङ्ख्येय वासनाभिश्चित्रमपि परार्थं संहत्य कारित्वात्

tad asaṅkhyeya vāsanābhiḥ citram api para arthaṃ saṃhatya kāritvāt

"that, countless, mental impressions, variegated, although, other, purpose, combination, because of acting"

Here Patañjali discusses the mind some more. He says that it has countless and variegated vāsanās/saṃskāras, although it has another purpose. He's clarifying II.18 where he said that the purpose of the seen (citta) is to provide experience and liberation. Remember that saṃskāras are mental impressions and there's one for every thought or experience you've had during the multitude of lives you've had, so there are a countless number of them, and we want to get rid of them (I.50 and I.51). However, he says here that the mind's purpose is for another, the puruṣa, because it acts in combination with the senses, sense objects, etc. This statement is an assumption in Sāṃkhya 17, where it states that "all aggregates exist for the purpose of something else" (and the something else must be for puruṣa), and in 31 where it says "The purpose of puruṣa is the only motive for their (buddhi, ahaṃkāra, and manas) activities."

The argument about aggregates existing for another purpose goes as follows: if parts are put together into something that will do something, there's a reason for putting them together, and that purpose is not for the parts, or the aggregate of the parts for that matter. For example, the parts of a car all come together to make a car, acting together, but the purpose of the car is not for the car itself, but for a person, who is obviously not the car, to move from place to place. The mind, senses, sense objects, (all prakṛti) in the argument above, come together for a purpose, and the purpose can't be for them, but for something else, and that something else must be the puruṣa, since puruṣa is the only other thing than prakṛti.

But what is the purpose of the puruṣa? The puruṣa cannot change, it's just pure consciousness, it can't have desires, because fulfilling a desire would entail change. A purpose needs a desire. Sāṃkhya says the purpose of the puruṣa is to be emancipated, but in 62 it says that prakṛti is never actually bound, and also never liberated. In 63, it says that prakṛti, not puruṣa, binds itself, and also liberates itself, for the sake of puruṣa.

I think that the nomenclature is confusing here, because that the only 'thing' with a purpose is the citta (mind), and that purpose is to get rid of pain and suffering, as noted by Patañjali in II.15 and II.16, and according to Patañjali, the way to get rid of pain and suffering is to get mokṣa. I suppose it could be said that the purpose of the citta is the same as the purpose of the puruṣa, but that seems to be a stretch.

IV.25 विशेष दर्शिन आत्म भाव भावना विनिवृत्ति:

viśeṣa darśinaḥ ātma bhāva bhāvanā vinivṛttiḥ
"different, seeing, self, state of being, investigating, stopping"

In this sūtra Patañjali continues on discussing the mind. He says that when you see the difference between the self (puruṣa) and your state of being (mind), you stop investigating into the nature of the self; once you understand this difference, there's nothing left to know. This is an addition to what he said in II.25 where he said that when you remove your avidyā (ignorance), the conjunction between the puruṣa and prakṛti is removed. This is kaivalyam. In II.26 he follows up, saying that the way to kaivalyam (liberation) is continuous viveka khyātiḥ (discriminative wisdom). See II.25 for a discussion of the difference between kaivalyam and mokṣa. You get this knowledge by going through the levels of samprajñāta samādhi discussed in I.17 and I.42 – I.44.

IV.26 तदा विवेक निम्नं कैवल्य प्राग्भारं चित्तम्

tadā viveka nimnam kaivalya prāgbhāram cittam
"then, wisdom, inclined toward, liberation, gravitates to, mind"

Continuing on the topic of the mind, Patañjali says that, with the wisdom mentioned in the previous sūtra, the mind is inclined toward discriminative wisdom (viveka khyātiḥ), and gravitates to kaivalyam. At this point, your mind is naturally attracted to viveka khyātiḥ and because of that it is also attracted to, and goes toward, liberation. Patañjali continues on this in the next sūtra.

Some commentaries have the word 'hi', meaning 'indeed', after 'tadā', meaning 'then', and some do not.

IV.27 तच्छिद्रेषु प्रत्ययान्तराणि संस्कारेभ्यः

tat chidreṣu pratyaya antarāṇi saṃskārebhyaḥ

"that, gap, contents of the mind, other, saṃskāras"

Here Patañjali says that the gaps/interruptions in the contents of the mind are caused by other saṃskāras. The other contents of the mind he's talking about here are ideas caused by saṃskāras other than discriminative wisdom ones. This is a followup on II.26 where he said that the way to kaivalyam (liberation) is continuous viveka khyātiḥ (discriminative wisdom). In II.26 he just said that continuous viveka khyātiḥ allows you to attain mokṣa, and here he explains that there are gaps where you lose that knowledge sometimes so that it's not continuous.

Just because discriminative wisdom has been acquired doesn't mean that all of your saṃskāras have been removed, and these saṃskāras sometimes remove the viveka khyātiḥ. So, as you go along on your sādhana getting rid of saṃskāras, these interruptions become less frequent and also don't last as long.

Examples of causes of the interruptions are, according to Vyāsa, are thoughts of 'I', 'mine', 'I am knowing', and 'I am not knowing'.

IV.28 हानमेषां क्लेशवदुक्तम्

hānam eṣāṃ kleśavat uktam

"removing, these, same as the kleśas, said"

Patañjali continues with saying that removing the saṃskāras mentioned in the previous sūtra is the same as removing the kleśas. Kleśas cause saṃskāras, as discussed before. Remember that the kleśas are never actually destroyed or removed. They are just rendered inoperative: made to be like roasted seeds that can never sprout. This is done by meditation, i.e. samādhi (II.11).

IV.29 प्रसङ्ख्यानेऽप्यकुसीदस्य सर्वथा विवेक ख्यातेर्धर्म मेघः समाधिः

prasaṅkhyāne api akusīdasya sarvathā viveka khyāteḥ dharma meghaḥ
    samādhiḥ
"highest knowledge, even, indifferent, always/permanent, discrimina-
    tion, wisdom, virtue, cloud, samādhi"

Here Patañjali says that when one is indifferent even to the highest knowledge (omniscience), this brings about permanent discriminative wisdom (viveka khyātiḥ) in the samādhi known as the cloud of virtue (dharma megha). Vyāsa says that because of the removal of the kleśas the mind stops and the yogī gets into the samādhi known as the cloud of virtue. In II.26 Patañjali said that uninterrupted discriminative wisdom (viveka khyātiḥ) is what you need to attain liberation/mokṣa, so here he's adding to the discussion in that section.

The various commentators don't discuss which of the levels of sampra-jñāta samādhi in I.17 and I.42 – I.44 correspond to dharma megha samādhi, as pointed out by Bryant, but it seems reasonable that it's nirvicāra samādhi, the highest level (see I.48 – I.50). See Appendix E for issues with the levels of samādhi.

IV.30 ततः क्लेश कर्म निवृत्तिः

tataḥ kleśa karma nivṛttiḥ
"therefore, kleśas, karma, disappearance/destruction/cessation"

In this sūtra Patañjali says that therefore, from the previous sūtra, you get the disappearance/destruction of the kleśas and karma. Here he's adding to his discussion of II.2 – II.13. In II.2 – II.10 he described the kleśas, in II.12 he said that karma is caused by the kleśas, and in II.13 he said as long as the kleśas exist you have karma and will be reborn. In II.11 he said that you get rid of the kleśas by meditation (samādhi). In the previous sūtra he said that indifference to the omniscience you get from samādhi gives you uninter-rupted, and permanent, viveka khyātiḥ, which allows you to attain mokṣa. Remember that you need to get rid of the kleśas and karma to attain mokṣa.

Vyāsa says in his commentary on this one that once the kleśas and karma are removed, the yogī is a jīvanmukta – liberated while alive. I disagree with this and discuss the concept of jīvanmukti in Appendix C.

IV.31 तदा सर्वावरण मलापेतस्य ज्ञानस्यानन्त्याज्ज्ञेयमल्पम्

tadā sarva āvaraṇa mala apetasya jñānasya ānantyāt jñeyam alpam
"then, all, obstructing, impurities, that which is removed, knowledge, infinite, to be learned, little"

Here Patañjali says, then, for one who has removed all the obstructing/ obscuring impurities (rajas and tamas), knowledge is infinite, and what's left to learn is little. This is an addition to IV.23 where he said that the buddhi knows all objects. There's always some rajas and tamas even if it's essentially nothing. The amount of rajas and tamas left is so small that Patañjali says 'all'. The buddhi is very sattvic, so once these have been removed from the buddhi, its knowledge is infinite. Bryant points out that the nature of sattva is knowledge and illumination, and when all rajas and tamas are removed, the knowledge and illumination of sattva is not impeded anymore and becomes limitless, so you get omniscience.

IV.32 ततः कृतार्थानां परिणाम क्रम समाप्तिर्गुणानाम्

tataḥ kṛta arthānāṃ pariṇāma krama samāptiḥ guṇānām
"therefore, done, of the purpose, transformation, sequence, termination,
   of the guṇas"

In this sūtra Patañjali gives more information about asamprajñāta samādhi. He says, therefore, since from the previous two sūtras you've removed the kleśas and your karma, and you know everything, the purpose of transformation of the guṇas is done, and the sequence of activities/changes of the guṇas are terminated.

Remember in II.18 Patañjali said that the purpose of prakṛti is to give liberation or experience. Since yogīs aren't interested in experience, for them its purpose is to give liberation. Also, in II.15 he said that the guṇas are always changing, thus causing everything to be painful. Then in II.22 he said that for the yogī whose purpose is complete, prakṛti ceases to exist for that yogī. In this sūtra he adds that the guṇas stop changing when their purpose is complete. Although the guṇas don't actually ever stop changing, to the yogī who has attained mokṣa, they have stopped changing since the puruṣa is disconnected from prakṛti.

IV.33 क्षण प्रतियोगी परिणामापरान्त निर्ग्राह्यः क्रमः

 kṣaṇa pratiyogī pariṇāma apara anta nirgrāhyaḥ kramaḥ

"moment, counterpart/correlation, transformation, nothing after, end, without being observed, sequence"

Here Patañjali says that the moments of small, sequential, transformations of a sequence are not observed until they end. He's defining a sequence (krama) from the previous sūtra, saying that it is a sequence of moments of transformations. He says that you don't notice the changes until the sequence ends. For example, you may buy a new sweatshirt, and it's your favorite, so you wear it all the time. You don't notice that it's getting old until all of a sudden, you see that it's old, frayed, and full of holes.

Vyāsa goes on to say that, while the transformations of the guṇas of the buddhi end upon attaining mokṣa, the transformations of the guṇas in general never end because that's the essence of the guṇas. This seems to be a clarification of II.22 where Patañjali said that, while prakṛti ceases to exist for the yogī that has attained mokṣa, it still exists for others.

IV.34 पुरुषार्थ शून्यानां गुणानां प्रतिप्रसवः कैवल्यं स्व रूप प्रतिष्ठा वा चिति शक्तेरिति

puruṣa artha śūnyānāṃ guṇānāṃ pratiprasavaḥ kaivalyam sva rūpa
   pratiṣṭhā vā citti śakteḥ iti

"puruṣa, purpose, devoid of, of the guṇas, return to the original state,
   liberation, own, form, established, or, consciousness, power, thus"

This is the final sūtra of Patañjali, and he says that the when the purpose of the puruṣa is complete, and it's devoid of the guṇas, which have returned to their original state, the puruṣa is established in its own form – consciousness power, and is liberated. At this point, the buddhi has disconnected from the puruṣa, and the puruṣa, separated from prakṛti and the guṇas, is liberated. Prakṛti, now disconnected from puruṣa, 'returns to its own state' (goes back into primordial prakṛti). This is a restating of I.3, where he said, then the seer (puruṣa) is established in its own form forever.

The last word in this sūtra 'iti' (thus) is his indication that it's the end of the text.

<u>Section Summary</u>

In summary, Patañjali talks about the buddhi, what it knows, and that, when it knows the difference between puruṣa and prakṛti, stops investigating on the nature of the puruṣa. Then it naturally gravitates towards mokṣa. At this point you've gotten rid of your kleśas and karma. Finally he discusses asamprajñāta samādhi and some things about what goes on when you attain mokṣa.

I'd like to point out here, again, that it's buddhi (which is prakṛti) that is liberated because it is now free from pain (II.15). So while you are dead at this point, since the body and mind, where the pain is felt is gone and cannot come back, and also because the body/mind is not your true self anyway, this is what the goal of yoga is, and what you have finally achieved. There is no change to the puruṣa.

<u>Chapter Summary</u>

In this chapter Patañjali addresses a number of different topics; more on the siddhis from the previous chapter, saṃskāras and karma and rebirth, properties of prakṛti and their association with the mind, comments on acquisition of knowledge, and finally more on attaining mokṣa. He finishes the chapter with some final thoughts on the buddhi and attaining mokṣa.

Appendix A Devanāgarī Pronunciation

Each box has the following:
- devanāgarī
- short or alternate form if exists
- transliteration
- pronunciation

Vowels							
अ a "about"	आ ा ā "twice as long as 'a'"	इ ि i "pit"	ई ी ī "street"	उ ु u "push"	ऊ ू ū "tool"	ए े e "hey"	ऐ ै ai "aisle"
ओ ो o "mole"	औ ौ au "how"	ऋ ृ ṛ "rim"	ॠ ॄ ṝ "r + ī as in reel"	ऌ ॢ ḷ "l followed by ṛ"	अं ङ ञ ṃ nasal mm or nn	अः aḥ	

Tongue position	Consonants					Sibilants	Semi vowels
Gutteral	क ka "<u>ka</u>rma"	ख kha "same as ka"[1]	ग ga "<u>g</u>all"	घ gha "same as ga"[1]	ङ ṅa "si<u>ng</u>"	ह ha "<u>h</u>a<u>l</u>t"	
Soft Palate	च ca "<u>ch</u>a<u>l</u>k"	छ cha "same as ca"[1]	ज ja "<u>J</u>apan"	झ jha "same as ja"[1]	ञ ña "pi<u>ñ</u>a<u>t</u>a"	श श्र[5] śa "<u>s</u>ure"	य ya "<u>y</u>awn"
Hard Palate	ट ṭa "<u>ta</u>boo"	ठ ṭha "same as ṭa"[1]	ड ḍa "<u>d</u>ark"	ढ ḍha "same as ḍa"[1]	ण ṇa "ti<u>nt</u>"	ष ṣa "<u>sh</u>op"	र प्र[2] र्प[3] "<u>ra</u>-port"
Back of the teeth	त ta n/a[4]	थ tha "same as ta"[1]	द da n/a[4]	ध dha "same as da"[1]	न na "<u>N</u>azi"	स sa "<u>sa</u>lami"	ल la "<u>la</u>ger"
Lips	प pa "<u>Pa</u>cific"	फ pha "same as pa"[1]	ब ba "<u>b</u>a<u>l</u>d"	भ bha "same as ba"[1]	म ma "<u>ma</u>chine"		व va "<u>v</u>anilla"

Some common compound letters	ज्ञ jña "gna", "gya", or "nya"	क्ष kṣa "ksha"	त्र tra "tra"	श्री śrī "shree"	ह्य hya "hya"		

1 These are pronounced with an exhale, but the 'h' is not pronounced.

2 The alternates for र is a diagonal line at the bottom of the character, e.g.

प्र is "pra". Note that the consonant can be any consonant, not just 'pa'.

3 The alternate for रृ is an arc above the line, e.g. अर्प is "arpa". Note that the consonant can be any consonant, not just 'pa'.

4 There are no English words like this.

5 The alternate for the श, which is श्च, is just the part above the च, i.e. just the top part of the character.

Appendix B Pronunciation of the Transliteration Marks

a = a as in about

ā = same as 'a' but twice as long

ai = ai as in aisle

au = ow as in how

b = b as in bald

bh = b in bald with an exhale

c = ch as in chalk

ch = ch as in chalk with an exhale

ḍ = d as in dark

ḍh = d as in dark with an exhale

d = same as ḍ but with the tongue on the back of the teeth

dh = same as ḍh but with the tongue on the back of the teeth and with an exhale

e = a as in hay

g = g as in gall

gh = g as in gall with an exhale

h = h as in halt

i = i as in pit

ī = ee as in street

j = j as in jump

jh = j as in Japan with an exhale

k = k as in karma

kh = k in karma with an exhale

l = l as in lager

m = m as in machine

n = n as in Nazi

ṇ = n as in tint

ṅ = n as in sing

ñ = ñ in piñata

o = o as in mole

p = p as in Pacific

ph = p as in Pacific with an exhale

r = r as in rat

ri = ri as in rip with rolled r

rī = ree as in reel with rolled r

s = s as in salami

ś = s as in sure

ṣ = sh as in shop

t = same as ṭ but with the tongue on the back of the teeth

ṭ = t as in taboo

th = same as ṭh but with the tongue on the back of the teeth and an exhale

ṭh = t as in taboo with an exhale

u = u as in push

ū = oo as in tool

v = v as in vanilla

y = y in yawn

jñ = 'gya', 'gna', or 'nya' depending on where in India you are from, e.g. samprajñāta is pronounced sampragnata or sampragyata or sampranyata.

Appendix C Thoughts on Jīvanmukti

The concept of jīvanmukti, or being liberated while alive, is an important one in Indic philosophies. Some philosophies accept it and some don't. Patañjali never mentions jīvanmukti but Vyāsa does, and he says that Patañjali supports it. I don't think that he does. Here's my thinking on it.

Bondage is defined as prakṛti and puruṣa being connected, so freedom from bondage is when they are disconnected, and that can only happen after you are dead.

Patañjali assumes the Sāṃkhya metaphysics, and in 67 of the Sāṃkhya Kārikā it says that once you get discriminating knowledge, dharma and the kleśas stop affecting the mind. Yet, one continues to have a body due to the force of saṃskāras, just like a potter's wheel continues to rotate while slowing down after the potter has stopped spinning it. Then in 68 it says that when you are separated from the gross body, prakṛti ceases to operate and you get kaivalyam which is both complete/absolute and final/permanent. This indicates that jīvanmukti is not possible since you don't get liberated until you leave the body, i.e. you're dead.

In Patañjali, in I.50 he says that from the ṛtambharā in I.48, you get saṃskāras that move you in direction of mokṣa, and those saṃskāras obstruct other saṃskāras that cause you to get enmeshed in prakṛtic thoughts. In I.51 he says that when you get rid of the samskaras that move you towards mokṣa, you get nirbīja samādhi (asamprajñāta samādhi). Vyāsa's comments say that in this state the samskaras that you have left keep your mind from fluctuating and getting enmeshed in prakṛti anymore. He says that the mind merges back into pradhāna, along with the samskaras, thus disconnecting from your puruṣa. He then says that the mind stops functioning, the puruṣa gets isolated in itself (disconnected from prakṛti), and is then called liberated. Again, you need to be dead to be liberated.

In his commentary on this sūtra, Hariharānanda says that asamprajñāta samādhi does not last forever, but you get samskaras that keep you going in the direction of kaivalyam. Then, he says, at some point your mind decides never to come back and that's when you get kaivalyam, or liberation. This is not supported by Patañjali since he specifically says that you get nirbīja samādhi when you get rid of all the samskaras. So therefore until you get rid of all the samskaras you aren't in asamprajñāta samādhi.

Patañjali, in II.25, says that removal of avidyā removes the conjunction between puruṣa and prakṛti, and this is kaivalyam. Since the conjunction has to exist when you are alive, it can only be removed when you are dead. Again, Patañjali does not support jīvanmukti.

The last place in Patañjali where jīvanmukti is referenced is in IV.30, where he says that, from permanent discriminative wisdom mentioned in IV.29, the kleśas, and karma cease. Vyāsa says that when this happens the yogī is a jīvanmukti, or liberated while alive. However, Patañjali doesn't say that.

Rāmānuja, in his commentary of the Vedānta Sūtras, (see Thibaut, page 118) rejects the idea of jīvanmukti. He says that the definition of Release (mokṣa) is "Release of a soul while connected to a body." He goes on to say that "You have yourself proved by scriptural passages that 'bondage' means the being joined to a body, and 'release' being free from a body!" Then he says "if the consciousness of the unreality of the body puts an end to embod-iedness, how can you say that jivanmukti means release of a soul while joined to a body?" He finishes with "The conclusion to be drawn from all this is that Release, which consists in the cessation of all Plurality, cannot take place as long as a man lives."

So, it seems to me that you aren't actually liberated until after there is a separation of prakṛti from puruṣa. You may have discriminative wisdom (viveka khyātiḥ) while alive, but you aren't actually liberated until after separation. Thus, jīvanmukti is not supported by Patañjali, or Sāṃkhya for that matter.

Appendix D Dualism, Non-dualism and Views on Mokṣa

First, I'll tackle dualism (dvaita) vs. non-dualism (advaita). In Indian philosophy, there are generally two metaphysical options, there is either only one fundamental thing, or type of thing, that exists, or exactly two. For example, Advaita Vedanta (Śaṃkaracarya) assumes that only Brahman exists and nothing else, whereas Sāṃkhya and Patañjali assume that there are two entities, puruṣa and prakṛti. Sāṃkhya and Patañjali can also be called pluralistic since there are an infinite number of puruṣas. Non-dualism really only applies to Advaita Vedanta, somewhat to Rāmānuja's Viśiṣṭādvaita (qualified non-dualism) philosophy, and to some flavors of Tantra. The first two are flavors of Vedanta. Dualism is pretty much all the other Indic philosophies, Sāṃkhya, Patañjali, Nyaya, Mimamsa, all the other flavors of Vedanta, etc., including Buddhism and Jainism.

One quirk that I've recently been aware of is that the terms dual and non-dual are used by some people in a different way than the philosophical way I described above. The other way is an experiential meaning, where non-dual is when a person or puruṣa experiences nothing other than themselves, and dualism is when the person is aware of things other than themselves. This is not the sense in which I'm using the term.

Of the various philosophies, only one is not a mokṣa tradition and that is Purva Mimamsa, which is all about doing and maintaining the ancient Vedic rituals. They want to use the rituals to get material things in this life, die and go to the celestial realms until their good karma has been used up, and get born again – forever.

All the rest of them are mokṣa traditions, where the idea is to get to a post-life state that's better than life, and never get reincarnated. The issue is that there are different ideas in the various philosophies as to what the mokṣa state is, and these views are affected by their ontologies. Next is a discussion of some various views on mokṣa with some comments on how their views are dependent on their ontology.

Sāṃkhya and Patañjali say that it's the state of kaivalyam, absolute aloneness; your puruṣa is still completely itself, but disconnected from prakṛti, and is only conscious of itself, in a state of bliss forever. This is a 'separation', as opposed to a 'union' philosophy in that you need to understand the difference between puruṣa and prakṛti to get mokṣa. Unfortunately, many people in the west don't like this idea, or they've never been exposed to it, and try to define what yoga is based on what they want. This is not yoga according to Patañjali.

Advaita Vedānta and some versions of Tantra say that mokṣa is merging with Brahman. In this scheme the individual puruṣa disappears after merging so that you don't exist as a separate entity anymore. These flavors of mokṣa are 'union' flavors. Rāmānuja's Viśiṣṭādvaita (qualified non-dualism) also says that Brahman is the only thing that exists, but that gods, puruṣas, and prakṛti, are real but are parts of Brahman. So while Brahman, according to this philosophy, is non-dual, there is a qualified non-duality in it.

Nyāya has a different definition of mokṣa. Many of you have probably heard of sat, chit, and ānanda, which are existence, consciousness, and bliss. Nyāya's view of mokṣa is just sat, which, means that while you exist forever, you aren't even conscious; a fairly hard thing to sell to people. This version of mokṣa is also a 'separation' flavor but different than Patañjali.

Bhakti is another version of mokṣa. The bhaktas, don't like any of the above versions of mokṣa, but want to have an eternal, loving, relationship with the divine. Absolute aloneness is not appealing because there's no relationship, neither is merging because again there's no relationship, and just 'sat' (being) is also not desired because you also can't have a relationship with the divine if you aren't even conscious.

So, from what I've said above, hopefully you now understand the 'union' vs. 'separation' viewpoints on mokṣa. You should also know that the overwhelming majority of Indic philosophies are dualistic, not non-dualistic.

One point that I would like to make here is that, Patañjali is usually ascribed to the title of 'yoga philosophy' where the other philosophies, in general, aren't. So when I hear someone talk about 'yoga' I assume that they are talking about Patañjali. Thus, to me, yoga is dualistic.

What I've said above is from reading many different texts and listening to many lectures. While I haven't studied most of the philosophies above in detail except for Sāṃkhya and Patañjali, I've done some reading on Advaita Vedānta and have superficially studied Nyaya.

The next point is why non-duality is so popular in the West. My thinking here is that it has to do with Vivekānanda and Yogānanda that came to the West in the late 1800s and early 1900s. Both of them were Advaita Vedāntists. These two gentlemen were highly influential Indian thinkers and this may explain why non-dualism is so prevalent in the west.

Appendix E Issues with I.42 – I.51

Patañjali is not consistent with his nomenclature. In I.17 he describes samprajñāta samādhi and gives it four levels: vitarka, vicāra, ānanda, and asmitā. Then in I.41 – I.44 he gives four different levels: savitarka, nirvitarka, savicāra, and nirvicāra. And he uses a different word for samādhi: samāpatti. Unfortunately he never talks about how these two sets of four levels relate or map to each other. One way to look at them is as follows:

```
vitarka samādhi  = savitarka samāpatti
??               = nirvitarka samāpatti
vicāra samādhi   = savicāra samāpatti
??               = nirvicāra samāpatti
ānanda samādhi = ??
asmitā samādhi  = ??
```

The problem with the above is that in I.43 he says that nirvicāra samāpatti is meditating on gross matter without words, etc. So it makes sense that he's adding a layer between vitarka and vicāra samādhi. Then in I.44 he says savicāra and nirvicāra are explained the same way. If we follow the same pattern as we did for vitarka and vicāra samādhi, then there's a new layer between vicāra and ānanda samādhi. Now we would have:

```
vitarka samādhi    = savitarka samāpatti
nirvitarka samādhi = nirvitarka samāpatti
vicāra samādhi     = savicāra samāpatti
nirvicāra samādhi  = nirvicāra samāpatti
ānanda samādhi    = ??
asmitā samādhi    = ??
```

The question immediately arises as to whether we need to add nirānanda and nirasmitā to the list. In fact, Vijñānabhikṣu did that in his commentary, but he's the only one that went there. All the other commentators don't add those two layers, mostly because Patañjali didn't mention them. So we can assume that they don't exist.

Swāmī Veda Bhārati introduces a unique idea here. He says that there are four samāpattis, savitarka, nirvitarka, savicāra, and nirvicāra. He thinks that the first three map to samādhis with the same name, but nirvicāra samāpatti includes nirvicāra, sa-ānanda, and sa-asmitā samādhi (see below). Patañjali never says this however, so, while it's an interesting idea, and it makes I.47 a bit more understandable, for the same reason that Patañjali didn't mention nirānanda and nirasmitā, we should be able to discard this idea.

vitarka samādhi   = savitarka samāpatti
nirvitarka samādhi = nirvitarka samāpatti
vicāra samādhi   = savicāra samāpatti
nirvicāra samādhi + ānanda samādhi + asmitā samādhi = nirvicāra samāpatti

The next facet of the problem is that in I.46 Patañjali says that the four samāpattis are all samādhi with seed (sabīja). So where do ānanda and asmitā samādhi fit? In I.47 he says that when you've perfected nirvicāra you get knowledge of the puruṣa. So if you get the knowledge of puruṣa in nirvicāra, then what are ānanda and asmitā for?

Unfortunately these questions don't have a good answer. In my opinion, the text has probably been modified over the past two thousand years, but we don't know. However, as I mentioned in the summary of section I.17, I.18, and I.41 – I.51, we can safely say that we need to go through some number of levels of samprajñāta samādhi to get the viveka khyātiḥ (discriminative wisdom) of the difference between puruṣa and prakṛti that we need to get to asamprajñāta samādhi, and then attain mokṣa.

Appendix F Sāṃkhya Metaphysics

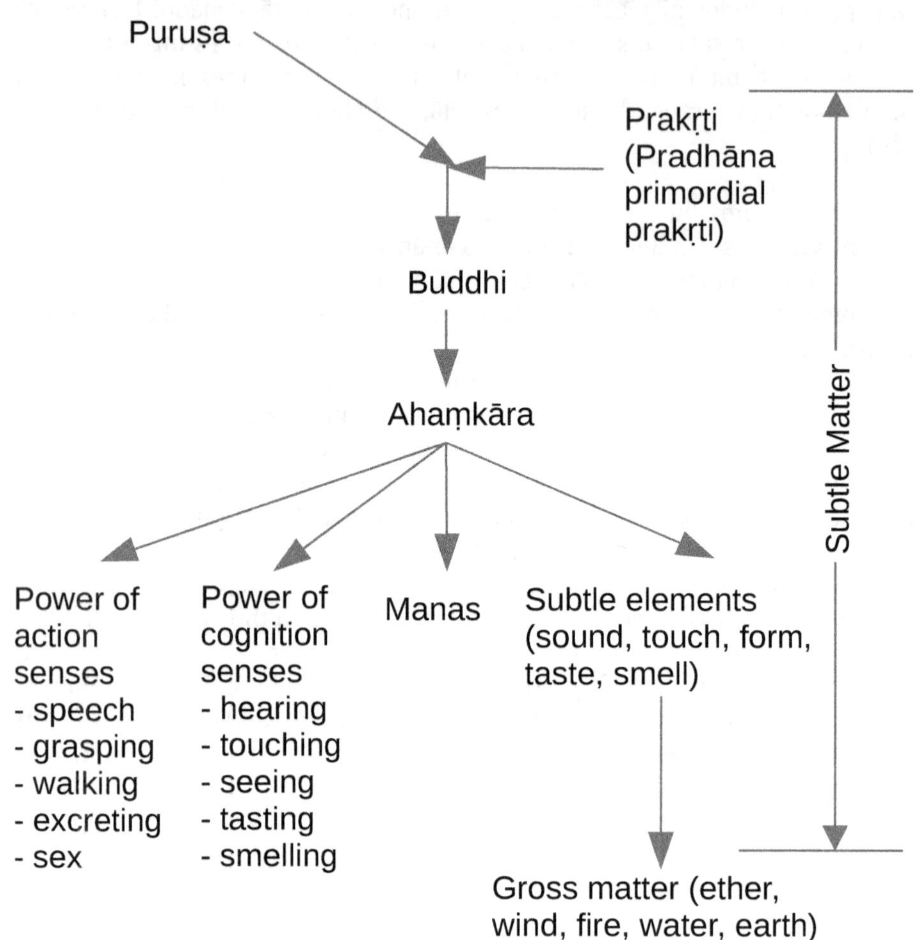

Appendix G Samāpatti vs Samādhi

Patañjali uses two different words when discussing the various levels of samprajñāta samādhi: samādhi and samāpatti. Unfortunately, it's not clear from his text what the difference is. The purpose of this appendix is to discuss what the difference, if any, there is between the two words.

In III.3 Patañjali says that samādhi is when during meditation the concept of "I am meditating on that" disappears and only the object of meditation is left. In I.46, and I.51 he uses the term 'samādhi' and in I.41-I.44 he uses the term 'samāpatti'. In I.17 he introduces the concept of samprajñāta samādhi (but doesn't use the word samādhi) and four levels of that, and in I.18 he introduces the 'other' (but doesn't say asamprajñāta samādhi). In I.46 he says that the previous levels are sabīja (with seed) samādhi. In I.51 he gives the final state of samādhi (nirbīja samādhi). In I.41 he introduces samāpatti, and in I.42 he introduces the term savitarka samāpatti, and then in I.43 he introduces nirvitarka, and then in I.44 he says that savicāra and nirvicāra are defined the same way as savitarka and nirvitarka. The sūtras mentioned above, and my translations, are listed below.

I.17 samprajñāta consists of the four levels, with physical awareness, absorption with subtle awareness, absorption with bliss, and absorption with the sense of I-ness (vitarka, vicāra, ānanda, asmitā).

I.18 The other is preceded by practice/abhyāsa, and has only latent saṃskāras remaining.

I.41 Samāpatti is when the mind has no vṛttis, i.e. is not fluctuating, it becomes just like a transparent jewel, taking the color of whatever it's placed on, whether the object is the knower, the instrument of knowledge, or the object of knowledge.

I.42 Savitarka-samāpatti, is on physical/gross objects with words, meaning, and knowledge.

I.43 Nirvitarka is without words, meaning, and ideas. It occurs when memory has been completely purified and the mind is empty of its own nature, and only the object shines forth.

I.44 By this alone, the states with "subtle awareness" (savicāra) and without "subtle awareness," (nirvicāra) whose objects are subtle matter, are explained.

I.45 The above-mentioned states are samādhi with seed.

I.46 Of those [samskaras from the previous sūtra], upon the cessation, nirbīja-samādhi, [seedless samādhi].

III.3 Samādhi is when the "I am meditating" disappears and the only thing in your mind is the object of meditation.

The question then, is what is the difference, if any, between samāpatti and samādhi? Why did Patañjali use two different terms? Below are a number of various translations followed by my conclusions.

Bryant – "Although samāpatti, introduced in this sūtra (I.41) for the first time, and samādhi can be correlated in a general way and the states of mind they represent overlap, they are not technically synonymous: Vijñānabhikṣu points out that the various types of samāpatti occur as results of samprajñāta-samādhi. Samādhi in general might best be understood in terms of the goal of yoga: the state when all vṛttis of the mind have been stilled. Samāpatti is, more specifically, the complete identification of the mind with the object of meditation. Put simply, the former is the more general or overall state of the stilled mind, the latter the more specific content or object upon which the mind has settled itself in order to become still. Complete mental identification with and absorption in an object, by definition, can obviously occur only when all other vṛttis have been stilled and the mind is without distraction; hence samāpatti occurs only in the context of samādhi as indicated in this sūtra."

Vyāsa – He has a long one too but I'm going to just take the part that I think is relevant. "This sort of resting of the mind in and its shaping after the receiver, the instrument of reception and the object received, viz. The Grahita (empiric self), the senses, and the elements, like a reflecting crystal, is called samāpatti or engrossment."

Hariharānanda – "The concentration attained in a habitually one-pointed mind is called engrossment or samāpatti. That is how samāpatti differs from simple concentration. The knowledge acquired in such a state of engrossment is Samprajñāna or complete knowledge or samprajñāta-yoga or concentration which gives complete and sustained knowledge."

Swāmī Veda Bhārati – "Samāpatti , the proficiency, attainment and transmutation of the mind, is the wisdom (prajñā) thus gained as derived from samprajñāta and is technically defined in I.17

Śaṃkaracarya – Identification-in-samādhi (samāpatti) is when the mental process has dwindled and the mind rests on either the knower

or the knowing process or a known object, and like a crystal apparently takes on their respective qualities."
Feuerstein – He translates samāpatti as "coincidence". He also doesn't discuss the word samāpatti at all.
Satchidānanda – He translates samāpatti as samādhi.
Dr. Jayaraman – He says that the two words are interchangeable.
Taimni – He doesn't discuss the difference between the two words. He just gives a long-winded description of samādhi.
Prabhavānanda – He translates samāpatti as samādhi.

Most of the commentators don't discuss the difference between the two words, in fact several of them translate samāpatti as samādhi. Hariharānanda says that samāpatti is the concentration, whereas samādhi is the knowledge gained during the concentration. Swāmī Bhārati seems to be diametrically opposite to Hariharānanda. Bryant seems to be saying that samādhi is the state of the stilled mind, while samāpatti is the object (or identification with?) in samādhi. There doesn't seem to be a general agreement as to the difference between the words, and many seem to agree that they are synonymous.

It's interesting that the entire chapter is about samādhi, in fact the name of the chapter is 'Samādhi Pāda'. He only uses the word samāpatti twice. Another point for samāpatti and samādhi being the same is that in I.46 Patañjali says that I.41 – I.45 are samādhi with seed; this includes the ones where he used the word samāpatti. I found an interesting statement in the *Cologne Digital Sanskrit Dictionaries: Edgerton Buddhist Hybrid Sanskrit Dictionary,* in the definition of samāpatti, "The fact seems to be that these two words [samāpatti and samādhi] are fundamentally and substantially identical in meaning, and that the attempts to differentiate are scholastic pedantry."

The issue with samādhi and samāpatti being the same is that in sūtra writing the words are supposedly meticulously selected to give a particular meaning, and using two words that mean the same goes against that notion. On the other hand, if they are different then Patañjali doesn't seem to do a good job in describing the differences.

Another thought that came from a lecture by Bryant is that it's possible that Patañjali just used different words to keep the text interesting. This is certainly a possibility and the answer that makes the most sense, so I believe the two words are synonymous. A final possibility is that at some point 'samādhi' was accidentally changed to 'samāpatti'. There is also merit to this idea since there are differences in the sūtras at some points between the commentators.

Appendix H Prana

A question that comes up frequently is "What is prāṇa?" Is it puruṣa, prakṛti, or something else? Prāṇa is important in the yoga paradigm, but what it is isn't discussed much; it's not really obvious what it is. Patañjali doesn't discuss it and neither does Sāṃkhya, but there are indications of the answer in those two places. I'm only going to discuss prāṇa as it pertains to Patañjali, i.e. whether it's puruṣa, prakṛti, or something else.

Prāṇa is frequently described as the 'life force', which doesn't seem like it's prakṛti since the word 'force' doesn't seem to imply subtle or gross matter. But it also doesn't seem like it's puruṣa because it's not the 'self'. So maybe it's something else? If so, what exactly is it?

Patañjali doesn't define prāṇa; in fact, he only mentions it in 7 sūtras, I.34, II.29, and II.49 – II.53, and then only in terms of prāṇāyāma. In I.34 he says that doing prāṇāyāma will give you mental equilibrium. In II.29 he just lists prāṇāyāma as one of the limbs of yoga. In II.49 – II.53 he discusses prāṇāyāma, but doesn't really talk about prāṇa.

The Sāṃkhya Kārikā also doesn't reference prāṇa. However, it does give some insight into the question. In 3, it says that prakṛti is not created, i.e. always exists, but it does generate the various tattvas/entities in the Sāṃkhya devolution tree. In the same sūtra it says that puruṣa is also not created, however, it doesn't generate anything, which is different from prakṛti. It doesn't say that prāṇa is not created, implying that it is created.

In 11, Sāṃkhya says that prakṛti (both manifest and the unmanifest pradhāna) consists of the guṇas, which are ultimately the same, in terms of being objective, non-conscious, and productive. Puruṣa is said to be the opposite; it's pure unchanging consciousness. In these two sūtras, Sāṃkhya is defining the fundamental entities of the philosophy. The point of this is to say that the only two things that always exist are puruṣa and prakṛti, so therefore prāṇa must be one of these two.

Swāmī Niranjanānanda Saraswatī, in his book Prāṇa Prāṇāyāma Prāṇa Vidya, notes that "prāṇa" is made up of two syllables, 'pra' and 'na', which denotes constancy, being a force in constant motion. In the introduction of the book, he discusses kuṇḍalinī śakti (a subtle energy that sits at the bottom of the spine and is coiled three and half times). In that discussion he says that prāṇa is both macrocosmic and microcosmic, so it must be manifest. Since puruṣa is not manifest, prāṇa must be prakṛti. He also discusses prāṇa śakti (śakti means force or energy), and says that it manifests as the cakras; this is another indication that prāṇa is prakṛti.

He also says that, according to Vedānta, there are two parts to our existence, prāṇa and consciousness. He says that consciousness is puruṣa, which means 'that which sleeps in the city'. He goes on to say that prāṇa is prakṛti, which means 'activity'.

So the conclusion is that prāṇa is prakṛti and not something else. It's not something else because the philosophy only has two uncreated, entities: puruṣa and prakṛti. And, as shown above, since only prakṛti creates/ generates, prāṇa must be created from praṇidhāna (primordial prakṛti). Finally, because prakṛti continually changes, whereas puruṣa doesn't change, prāṇa must be prakṛti.

Bibliography

Edwin Bryant "The Yoga sūtras of Patañjali" 2009

Edwin Bryant – Various workshops and lectures in 2020 – 2022.

Vachapati Mishra (Translation by Rama Prasada) "Patañjali's Yoga Sūtras" 2010

Swāmī Hariharānanda Āranya "Yoga Philosophy of Patañjali" 1983

Swāmī Veda Bhārati (aka Pandi Usharbudh Arya) "Yoga Sūtras of Patañjali" Study material version. No date.

Swāmī Veda Bhārati "Yoga sūtras of Patañjali" Volume II 2004

Sri Swāmī Satchidānanda "The Yoga Sūtras of Patañjali" 2007

Salvatore Zambito "The Unadorned Thread of Yoga" 1992

Swāmī Niranjanānanda Saraswati "Sāṃkhya Darśana" 2008

Swāmī Niranjanānanda Saraswati "Prāṇa Prāṇāyāma Prāṇa Vidya" 1998

Yogānanada "Autobiography of a Yogī" 2004

Discussions with Indubala Bhardwaj (my teacher)

Patrick Olivelle "The Early Upanishads" 1998

Vicki MacKenzie "Cave in the Snow" 1998

Georg Feuerstein "The Yoga-Sutra of Patañjali" 1989

Bibliography

Trevor Leggett "Sankara on the Yoga Sutras" 2006

I.K. Taimni "The Science of Yoga" 2010

Swāmī Prabhavanda and Christopher Isherwood "How to know God. The Yoga Aphorisms of Patañjali" 1969

Audio recording of Dr. Jayaraman from Mysore India. Date unknown.

Sri Sri Ravi Shankar "Celebrating Silence" (page 6). 2014.

George Thibaut "The Vedanta Sutras With The Commentary By Ramanuja" No published date in the book.

Cologne Digital Sanskrit Dictionaries: Edgerton Buddhist Hybrid Sanskrit Dictionary

Glossary

abhiniveśaḥ – The fifth of the five kleśas: the fear of death, or clinging to life.

abhyāsa – Practice. One of the two things, the other being vairāgya (non-attachment/dispassion), that you need to do to get rid of vṛttis.

āgama – The third of the three valid source of knowledge: testimony.

āgāmin – Karma that you have done in the current life that you will experience later.

ahaṃkāra – One of the three parts of the citta: ego, or the sense of 'I'.

ahiṃsā – One of the yamas (ethical restraints). Non-harming.

ākāśa – One of the five gross elements (mahā bhūtas): space/ether.

akliṣṭa – One of the two types of vṛttis: helpful or non-painful.

aṇimā – One of the siddhis: the power to become very small.

antarāya – obstacle/disturbance/obstruction. In this text they are the obstacles to samādhi.

anumāna – The second of the three valid sources of knowledge: inference.

ap – One of the five gross elements (mahā bhūtas): water.

apāna – One of the five major types of prāṇa: downward force.

aparigraha – One of the yamas (ethical restraints): non acceptance of more than necessary.

asamprajñāta – The second of the two major types of samādhi: samādhi without a seed, or object.

āsana – The third of the eight limbs of Patañjali's Aṣṭāṅga yoga: posture.

asmitā – The second of the five kleshas: ego.

Aṣṭāṅga – The name of Patañjali's eight-limbed yoga philosophy.

asteya – One of the yamas (ethical restraints). Non stealing.

Āvaṭya – An ancient sage.

avidyā – The first of the five kleśas: ignorance.

Bhagavad Gītā – The Bhagavad Gītā; the Lord's Song. A scriptural and yogic text.

Bhārati – A commentator on the Patañjali sūtras.

bhāvanam – Cultivating.

bhūta – Any one of the five types of gross matter: space, wind, fire, water, earth.

bīja – seed.

brahmacarya – One of the yamas (ethical restraints): celibacy.

buddhi – The part of the mind/citta that is the discriminator.

citta – The mind 'stuff'. It consists of the buddhi, ahaṃkāra, and manas.

Dakṣa – The father of Satī, the previous incarnation of Pārvatī. Both were married to Śiva.

devanāgarī – The set of characters of the Saṃskṛtam (Sanskrit) language.

dhāraṇā – The sixth of the eight limbs of Patañjali's Aṣṭāṅga Yoga: concentration.

dharma – The things you need to do as part of your duty in this lifetime.

dhyāna – The seventh of the eight limbs of Patañjali's Aṣṭāṅga Yoga: meditation.

draṣṭṛ – The seer: the puruṣa.

dṛśya – The seen: anything in prakṛti.

dveṣa – The fourth of the five kleśas: aversion.

gandha – One of the subtle elements (tanmātras): smell.

Gaṇeśa – A Hindu deity, the son of Śiva.

gṛhastha – The second of the four stages of life: householder.

guṇa – Any of the three qualities of prakṛti: sattva, rajas, and tamas.

hāna – cessation.

Hanūmān – The Hindu monkey god. A major character in the Rāmāyaṇa.

Hariharānanda – Swāmī Hariharānanda Āraṇya. A commentator on the Patañjali sūtras.

ida nadī – One of the nadīs or subtle energy channels in the body.

īśitṛtva – One of the siddhis: ability to control outward appearance, disappearance, and rearrangement of elements

iṣṭa devatā – A person's preferred deity.

Īśvara – The Lord/the divine. A special puruṣa according to Patañjali.

japa – Repeating a mantra.

Jaigīśavya – An ancient sage.

jñāna – knowledge.

kaivalya – Patañjali's definition of mokṣa. A permanent post-life state of bliss, which means absolute aloneness.

karma – Literally 'action'. Karma that you do in this life affects the species, lifespan, and pain/pleasure in future lives.

karmāśaya – The repository of karma. Where actions that the person hasn't experienced the fruit/results of are stored until they can be experienced.

khyātiḥ – Wisdom. Usually used as part of 'viveka khyātiḥ': discriminative wisdom.

kleśa – Obstacle/impediment. There are five: ignorance, ego, attraction, aversion, and fear of death.

kliṣṭa – One of the two types of vṛttis: non-helpful or painful.

Kriyā – Kriyā Yoga, which consists of asceticism/effort, study, and surrender to Īśvara.

krama – sequence.

kriyamāṇa – Karma you are getting the fruit of right now or in the immediate future.

Kṛṣṇa – The Hindu deity who was one of the major characters in the Bhagavad Gītā.

kṣatriya – One of the four classes of people in India: a ruler and/or warrior.

kūrma – Tortoise. Mentioned in the text as one of the nadīs: energy channels in the body.

kuśa – A type of grass mentioned in the Bhagavad Gītā as one layer of what to sit on when meditating.

laghimā – One of the siddhis: the ability to be very light and to fly.

mahā – Great.

mahā bhūtas – Gross matter. There are five types: space, wind, fire, water, earth.

mahimā – One of the siddhis: the ability to become large and heavy.

manas – The part of the mind/citta that interfaces with the senses.

mantra – Chant. Part of Kriyā Yoga, the part svādhyāya.

mokṣa – Liberation: A permanent post-life state that is better than being alive, and involves not being reborn. The goal of yoga. Patañjali's definition of mokṣa is kaivalyam, or absolute aloneness.

nadī – One of the 72,000 subtle energy channels in the body.

Nirodha – Stopping.

niyama – The second limb of the eight limbs of Patañjali's Aṣṭāṅga Yoga: observances and attitudes a yogī should have.

Nyāya – One of the six darśanas/visions/philosophies of India: a cosmology based on logic and inference.

pāda – Foot. Used in this text as a synonym for chapter.

pariṇāma – Transformation. Patañjali mentions three: nirodha, samādhi, and ekāgrata.

Pārvatī – The reincarnation of Satī. After doing 4000 years of tapas to attract Śiva, she became his consort.

Patañjali – The author of the Patañjali Sūtras, the philosophy of yoga.

piṅgala nadī– One of the nadīs or subtle energy channels in the body.

pradhāna – Primordial prakṛti before being touched by puruṣa.

prakāmya – One of the siddhis: the power of irresistible will (can go through solid rock, unable to be immersed in water, etc.)

prakṛti – Matter. Everything other than puruṣa. One of the two ontological entities that always exists.

prakṛti-laya – Enmeshed in prakṛti. One of two types of puruṣas that can get to samādhi by being born.

pramāṇa – One of the five types of vṛttis: right/correct knowledge.

prāṇa – The life force. Also a collection of types of energy. The five major types are prāṇa, apāna, samāna, udāna, and vyāna.

prāṇāyāma – The fourth limb of the eight limbs of Patañjali's Aṣṭāṅga Yoga: expansion of prāṇa in the body.

praṇidhāna – Two words, 'prani' which means 'to offer', and 'dhana' which is 'anything that is of value to you', or 'your dearest treasure'. Īśvara praṇidhāna is offering/surrendering your most precious treasure, i.e. yourself, to Īśvara.

prāpti – One of the siddhis: ability to reach anything desired no matter how far away.

prārabdha – Karma you are going to experience the fruit of in the current life.

pratiprasava – Going backwards. Associated with getting rid of the kleśas.

pratyāhāra – The fifth limb of the eight limbs of Patañjali's Aṣṭāṅga Yoga: withdrawal of the senses.

pratyakṣa – The first of the three valid sources of knowledge: direct perception.

pṛthvī – One of the five gross elements (mahā bhūtas): earth.

purāṇa – A type of ancient Hindu text.

puruṣa – The self. Pure consciousness. One of the two ontological entities in Sāṃkhya, and Patañjali's philosophy that always exists.

rāga – The fourth of the kleśas: aversion.

rāja – King. Rāja Yoga is one of the names of Patañjali's philosophy.

rajas – one of the three guṇas (qualities of prakṛti), meaning heat/activity.

Rāma – An incarnation of Viṣṇu, one of the Hindu deities. Rāma was one of the major characters in the Rāmāyaṇa.

Rāmāyaṇa – An ancient Hindu text containing the story of Rāma and Sītā.

rasa – One of the subtle elements (tanmātras): taste.

ṛtambharā – Truth bearing wisdom acquired in the higher stages of samprajñāta samādhi.

rūpa – One of the subtle elements (tanmātras): form.

sādhana – Your path/journey to mokṣa.

samādhi – The eighth limb of the eight limbs of Patañjali's Aṣṭāṅga Yoga. You need this to get the knowledge you need for mokṣa. In samādhi you lose the concept of 'I am meditating on that' and the only thing left is 'that'.

samāna – One of the five main pranas: responsible for digestion.

samāpatti – same as samādhi.

Sāṃkhya – One of the six darśanas (philosophies). Patañjali's philosophy is based on it and its metaphysics.

samprajñāta – One of the two main types of samādhi. It has multiple levels in it.

saṃskāra – Mental impression of a previous thought or experience.

Saṃskṛtaṃ – The language that Patañjali's philosophy was written in. Also called Sanskrit.

saṃyama – A shorthand way to represent going through dhāraṇā, dhyāna, and samādhi, that Patañjali uses when discussing the siddhis in chapter three.

saṃyoga – Another word for the conjunction of purusha and prakriti that you have when you have a body.

saṃnyāsa – The fourth of the four stages of life: complete renunciation. Saṃnyāsis are the wandering yogīs (sadhus) in India.

sañcita – Karma you have done and haven't yet experienced the fruit of yet, in the current or a future life.

Satchidānanda – A word that means reality, and consciousness, and bliss. Swāmī Satchidānanda was also a commentator on Patañjali.

Satī – Śiva's first consort. She used her prana to burn herself up when her father, Dakṣa, insulted Śiva.

satkāryavāda – The concept in Sāṃkhya that nothing is ever created: things are just changed from one thing to another.

sattva – one of the three guṇas (qualities of prakṛti), meaning light/peaceful/quiet.

satya – One of the yamas (ethical restraints): non lying.

śabda – One of the subtle elements (tanmātras): sound.

Śaṃkaracarya – An ancient philosopher.

śauca – One of the niyamas: purity.

siddhis – Super-normal powers from yogic practice.

Śiva – One of the Hindu deities. The name means 'auspicious one'.

śiṣya – The disciple of a guru.

Sītā – The wife of Rāma. One of the major characters in the Rāmāyaṇa.

śloka – A sentence/verse in a religious text, e.g. the Bhagavad Gītā, has 700 ślokas.

smṛti – The fifth of the five types of vṛttis: memory. Also, remembered scriptural knowledge as different from śruti (revealed knowledge from the divine). Traditionally, smṛti texts are not as important, as the śruti texts.

sparśa – One of the subtle elements (tanmātras): touch.

śruti – A text that is considered revealed knowledge from the divine, e.g. the Vedas.

subtle matter – The layers of the Sāṃkhya devolution tree (see Appendix F) between gross matter at the bottom, and pradhāna, at the top.

sūtra – A very terse 'sentence' in an Indic text written in the sūtra style of writing. The Patañjali Sūtras were written in this style.

svādhyāya – The second part of Kriyā Yoga: study. Traditionally it was study of scripture and chanting mantras.

tamas – one of the three guṇas (qualities of prakṛti), meaning inactivity/inertia/darkness.

tanmātra – Subtle matter. It devolves out of ahaṃkāra (ego) and the mahā bhūtas (gross matter) devolve out of it.

tapas – Heat, effort, austerity. The first part of Kriyā Yoga.

tejas – One of the five gross elements (mahā bhūtas): fire. Also means splendor.

udāna – One of the five main pranas: the upward force.

Vācaspati Miśra – An ancient commentator.

vairāgya – Non-attachment/dispassion. One of the two things, the other being abhyāsa (practice), that you need to do to get rid of vṛttis.

Vālmīki – Author of the Rāmāyaṇa.

vānaprastha – The third of the four stages of life: retirement and focus on spiritual practices.

varṇa – Literally 'color'. Used also to denote taxonomy. e.g. āśrama varṇa (the four stages of life), or one of the castes in Indian society.

vāsanā – Subtle saṃskāra.

vaśitva – One of the siddhis: ability to control the elements and their qualities, and control other beings.

vāyu – One of the five gross elements (mahā bhūtas): water.

vibhūti – Power. The name of the third chapter of the Patañjali Sūtras. Also the three lines of ashes Śaivites put on their foreheads.

vicāra – The second level of samprajñāta samādhi: samādhi with concepts.

videhā – Bodiless. These are very powerful yogīs that don't have a body.

Vijñānabhikṣu – An ancient commentator.

vipākaḥ – Used by Patañjali in his discussion on karma. It means the fruit of karma here.

viveka – Discrimination.

vṛtti – Fluctuation. In this text it refers to the fluctuations of the mind stuff that you need to get rid of to get to samādhi.

vyāna – One of the five main pranas: the force that is diffused throughout the body.

Vyāsa – The most important commentator on the Patañjali Sūtras. Also, he was the author of many very important Indic texts.

yama – The first limb of the eight limbs of Patañjali's Aṣṭāṅga Yoga: ethical restraints.

yatrakāmāvasāyitva – One of the siddhis: ability to manipulate the elements.

yogī – Anyone following the yogic path.

Word Index

This index is alphabetically ordered. However, words that start with diacritical marks, e.g. ā, occur after words that don't start with diacritical marks. So if you can't find the word you are looking for, look again near the end.

abhiniveśaḥ..58, 61, 191
abhyāsa.............................21, 22, 25, 34, 35, 44, 183, 191, 196
ahaṃkāra 8, 9, 15, 39, 44, 45, 46, 49, 70, 71, 72, 75, 102, 119, 124, 133, 134, 154, 161, 162, 191, 192, 196
ahiṃsā...82, 89, 191
akliṣṭa..18, 25, 44, 191
amādhi...107
aṇimā...133, 191
antarāya..32, 33, 34, 35, 191
anumāna...19, 51, 191
apāna..130, 191, 194
aparigraha...82, 84, 90, 191
asamprajñāta 17, 27, 28, 43, 44, 45, 49, 51, 52, 62, 67, 77, 107, 110, 138, 166, 168, 175, 181, 183, 191
asmitā. 43, 45, 47, 49, 58, 59, 62, 71, 109, 129, 132, 134, 145, 159, 180, 181, 183, 191
Aṣṭāṅga v, 11, 55, 56, 59, 68, 75, 79, 81, 95, 97, 102, 103, 105, 108, 115, 141, 191, 192, 193, 194, 195, 197
asteya...82, 83, 89, 191
avidyā.......58, 59, 61, 62, 68, 71, 76, 77, 78, 79, 151, 152, 160, 163, 176, 191
bharā..45, 50, 152, 194
bhāvanam...32, 87, 88, 89, 191
bhūta.....21, 44, 48, 70, 115, 119, 120, 122, 132, 133, 139, 191, 193, 194, 196
bīja.......................31, 43, 49, 52, 77, 110, 138, 175, 181, 183, 184, 191
brahmacarya...82, 83, 84, 90, 191
buddhi 1, 8, 9, 13, 15, 39, 44, 45, 46, 49, 50, 59, 60, 61, 67, 69, 70, 71, 72, 74, 75, 76, 78, 93, 102, 108, 116, 119, 120, 124, 127, 128, 132, 133, 134, 137, 138, 141, 153, 154, 158, 159, 160, 161, 162, 166, 167, 168, 169, 177, 191, 192
citta. 9, 13, 15, 16, 33, 37, 39, 56, 67, 102, 105, 106, 108, 111, 112, 121, 124, 127, 129, 145, 155, 156, 157, 159, 161, 162, 163, 191, 192, 193

Dakṣa...130, 192, 195
Darśana...7, 33, 59, 93, 126, 189, 193, 195
devanāgarī...1, 12, 170, 192
dhāraṇā......1, 11, 38, 44, 55, 81, 102, 105, 106, 107, 108, 109, 110, 111, 112, 113, 115, 119, 141, 192, 195
dharma..................................63, 115, 116, 117, 133, 149, 165, 175, 192
dhyāna 1, 11, 44, 55, 62, 81, 105, 106, 107, 108, 109, 110, 111, 112, 113, 115, 119, 141, 146, 192, 195
draṣṭṛ...70, 161, 192
dṛśya...192
dveṣa...58, 60, 61, 62, 192
gandha...72, 192
Gaṇeśa...192
gṛhastha..84, 192
guṇa......24, 25, 37, 39, 68, 70, 71, 72, 93, 105, 117, 121, 124, 144, 154, 166, 167, 168, 187, 192, 194, 195, 196
ida nadī...82, 100, 192
iṣṭa devatā..29, 94, 101, 192
Jaigīṣavya..121, 192
japa...32, 57, 87, 94, 171, 173, 192
jīvanmukta..93, 166
jñāna...19, 20, 40, 44, 47, 50, 79, 88, 119, 120, 121, 123, 124, 125, 126, 127, 130, 139, 140, 146, 166, 180, 184, 192, 196
karma....1, 11, 30, 32, 44, 55, 63, 64, 65, 70, 81, 88, 103, 105, 123, 143, 144, 145, 146, 149, 150, 151, 152, 165, 166, 168, 169, 171, 173, 176, 177, 191, 192, 193, 194, 195, 197
karmāśaya...64, 65, 146, 192
khyātiḥ......11, 45, 55, 57, 59, 68, 75, 78, 79, 81, 82, 109, 127, 137, 139, 141, 145, 151, 152, 160, 163, 164, 165, 176, 181, 192
kleśa....1, 21, 30, 33, 55, 57, 58, 59, 60, 61, 62, 63, 64, 65, 71, 76, 78, 79, 81, 103, 105, 129, 132, 138, 141, 146, 152, 164, 165, 166, 168, 175, 176, 191, 192, 194
kliṣṭa...18, 25, 44, 191, 193
krama...117, 123, 139, 140, 166, 167, 193
Kriyā....................1, 55, 56, 57, 62, 63, 70, 81, 89, 103, 105, 193, 196
Kṛṣṇa....................................30, 39, 60, 92, 97, 99, 149, 154, 193
kṣatriya..85, 193
kūrma...126, 193
kuśa...92, 193

laghimā...133, 193
mahā..........................44, 48, 52, 85, 130, 132, 133, 139, 191, 193, 194, 196
mahimā...133, 193
manas....8, 9, 13, 15, 34, 38, 44, 71, 75, 93, 102, 108, 124, 161, 162, 192, 193
mantra..23, 57, 87, 94, 138, 143, 192, 193, 196
mokṣa...1, 2, 5, 7, 9, 10, 11, 13, 15, 17, 18, 22, 23, 24, 25, 27, 30, 32, 43, 44, 45, 50, 51, 52, 53, 55, 57, 58, 59, 62, 63, 67, 69, 70, 73, 74, 75, 76, 77, 78, 79, 81, 87, 91, 92, 93, 94, 97, 98, 99, 101, 103, 105, 107, 108, 109, 115, 121, 128, 132, 135, 137, 138, 140, 141, 143, 145, 152, 155, 160, 161, 163, 164, 165, 167, 168, 169, 175, 176, 177, 178, 181, 192, 193, 194, 195
mṛti...196
nadī..38, 82, 100, 125, 126, 192, 193
niyama 1, 11, 55, 56, 81, 82, 83, 84, 86, 87, 89, 93, 95, 97, 103, 110, 193, 195
Nyāya...7, 178, 193
pāda...1, 3, 11, 13, 15, 55, 62, 105, 143, 185, 193
pariṇāma......1, 68, 105, 108, 111, 112, 113, 117, 119, 144, 154, 166, 167, 193
Pārvatī..130, 192, 193
piṅgala nadī..38, 82, 100, 193
pradhāna....................49, 50, 68, 71, 72, 75, 119, 135, 175, 187, 193, 196
prākāmya...133, 194
prakāśa..70, 101, 122, 132
prakṛti...1, 8, 13, 16, 17, 18, 24, 25, 27, 28, 29, 30, 31, 32, 43, 44, 45, 49, 50, 51, 53, 59, 62, 67, 68, 69, 70, 71, 72, 73, 74, 75, 76, 77, 78, 79, 83, 105, 107, 110, 115, 116, 117, 119, 121, 124, 129, 135, 137, 138, 139, 141, 143, 144, 145, 147, 149, 152, 153, 154, 155, 156, 157, 158, 160, 161, 162, 163, 167, 168, 169, 175, 176, 177, 178, 181, 187, 188, 192, 193, 194, 195, 196
prakṛti-laya...28, 29, 53, 143
prakṛtilaya...35
pramāṇa...19, 50, 51, 155, 194
prāṇa...............11, 38, 55, 81, 82, 99, 101, 103, 130, 187, 188, 189, 191, 194
prāṇāyāma. 1, iii, 11, 38, 41, 55, 81, 82, 97, 99, 100, 101, 102, 103, 110, 145, 187, 188, 189, 194
praṇidhāna............29, 30, 35, 43, 56, 57, 62, 81, 86, 87, 94, 95, 109, 188, 194
prāpti..133, 194
prārabdha...123, 194
pratiprasava...62, 168, 194
pratyāhāra.................................1, 11, 55, 81, 82, 97, 102, 103, 110, 194
pratyakṣa...19, 50, 194
pṛthvī..72, 194

purāṇa...130, 194
puruṣa 3, 8, 9, 10, 13, 16, 17, 18, 24, 25, 30, 31, 32, 43, 44, 45, 46, 50, 51, 52, 53, 59, 61, 62, 64, 67, 68, 69, 70, 71, 72, 73, 74, 75, 76, 77, 78, 79, 93, 107, 110, 116, 119, 127, 128, 129, 133, 137, 138, 141, 143, 152, 153, 154, 155, 156, 157, 158, 159, 160, 161, 162, 163, 167, 168, 175, 176, 177, 178, 181, 187, 188, 192, 193, 194
rāga...39, 58, 60, 61, 62, 152, 156, 194
rāja...25, 71, 121, 194
Rāma...32, 44, 194, 195
Rāmāyaṇa..3, 32, 192, 194, 195, 196
rasa................................12, 61, 62, 72, 138, 159, 165, 168, 189, 194
rūpa..................19, 43, 48, 72, 102, 107, 122, 132, 134, 150, 153, 168, 194
sādhana. 1, 2, 10, 18, 23, 25, 27, 28, 29, 33, 40, 44, 55, 57, 63, 67, 84, 90, 92, 141, 143, 149, 160, 164, 194
samādhi 1, 11, 13, 15, 16, 17, 25, 27, 28, 29, 35, 39, 43, 44, 45, 46, 47, 48, 49, 50, 51, 52, 53, 55, 56, 57, 59, 62, 67, 75, 77, 78, 81, 92, 94, 95, 99, 101, 103, 105, 106, 107, 108, 109, 110, 112, 113, 115, 119, 128, 131, 132, 135, 137, 138, 141, 143, 147, 152, 160, 163, 164, 165, 166, 168, 175, 180, 181, 183, 184, 185, 186, 191, 193, 194, 195, 196, 197
samāna...130, 194, 195
samāpatti..............................1, 46, 47, 98, 180, 181, 183, 184, 185, 186, 195
Sāṃkhya 1, 7, 8, 9, 30, 44, 48, 49, 67, 68, 72, 74, 75, 107, 116, 119, 120, 132, 134, 153, 154, 157, 161, 162, 175, 176, 177, 178, 182, 187, 189, 194, 195, 196
saṃnyāsa...84, 195
samprajñāta...27, 28, 43, 44, 45, 46, 47, 49, 51, 52, 62, 67, 77, 107, 109, 110, 137, 138, 160, 163, 165, 166, 168, 174, 175, 180, 181, 183, 184, 191, 194, 195, 196
saṃskāra.....1, 21, 27, 30, 44, 51, 52, 63, 68, 84, 89, 105, 111, 113, 121, 143, 144, 147, 149, 150, 151, 152, 155, 162, 164, 169, 175, 183, 195, 196
Saṃskṛtam.....................3, 6, vii, 9, 10, 12, 16, 18, 49, 76, 91, 139, 192, 195
saṃtoṣa...86
saṃyama.....107, 108, 109, 110, 113, 119, 120, 121, 122, 123, 124, 125, 126, 127, 131, 132, 134, 139, 159, 195
saṃyoga...70, 74, 76, 195
sañcita...123, 195
Satī...130, 192, 193, 195
satkāryavāda..116, 120, 153, 154, 195
satya...82, 83, 85, 89, 195

Sītā...32, 194, 195
smṛti...19, 21, 28, 31, 48, 150, 159, 196
sparśa...72, 196
subtle matter.....8, 24, 43, 45, 46, 48, 49, 71, 72, 75, 119, 122, 124, 132, 154, 183, 196
svādhyāya...v, 29, 56, 57, 62, 81, 86, 94, 193, 196
tanmātra....................44, 48, 49, 119, 122, 132, 133, 134, 192, 194, 195, 196
tapas.......................................56, 62, 81, 86, 87, 94, 101, 130, 193, 196
tejas..72, 196
udāna..130, 194, 196
vairāgya...23, 25, 33, 35, 60, 141, 191, 196
Vālmīki...196
vānaprastha...84, 196
varṇa...120, 196
vāsanā...149, 150, 151, 162, 196
vaśitva...133, 196
vāyu..72, 196
vibhūti...1, 105, 196
vicāra...................43, 45, 47, 48, 49, 50, 51, 52, 109, 165, 180, 181, 183, 196
videhā..27, 28, 29, 35, 53, 132, 143, 196
vipākaḥ..64, 197
viveka...11, 45, 50, 55, 57, 59, 68, 75, 78, 79, 81, 82, 92, 107, 109, 127, 137, 139, 140, 141, 145, 151, 152, 160, 163, 164, 165, 176, 181, 192, 197
vṛtti.....1, 15, 16, 18, 19, 20, 21, 22, 25, 27, 38, 43, 44, 46, 58, 62, 63, 67, 68, 100, 108, 124, 126, 132, 145, 152, 163, 165, 183, 184, 191, 193, 194, 196, 197
vyāna...130, 194, 197
yama. 11, 55, 56, 81, 82, 83, 84, 85, 86, 87, 89, 93, 95, 97, 99, 103, 108, 109, 110, 119, 120, 121, 122, 123, 124, 125, 126, 127, 131, 132, 134, 139, 159, 191, 193, 195, 197
yatrakāmāvasāyitva...133, 197
āgamāḥ...19
ākāśa..72, 131, 134, 191
ānanda..43, 45, 47, 49, 109, 178, 180, 181, 183
āsana......1, iii, v, 6, 11, 23, 55, 57, 81, 82, 97, 98, 99, 100, 103, 110, 145, 191
Āvaṭya...121, 191
īśitṛtva..133, 192
Īśvara..1, 27, 29, 30, 31, 32, 34, 35, 43, 53, 56, 57, 62, 74, 75, 81, 86, 87, 94, 95, 109, 161, 192, 193, 194

ṛṣi..39
ṛtaṃ...45, 50, 51, 52, 152, 194
ṛtambharā...45, 152, 175, 194
śabda...20, 47, 72, 120, 122, 195
Śaṃkaracarya...177, 184, 195
Śauca...86, 92, 93, 195
śiṣya...195
Śiva...57, 97, 101, 130, 192, 193, 195
śloka...v, 13, 39, 149, 196
śruti...31, 196

www.ingramcontent.com/pod-product-compliance
Lightning Source LLC
Chambersburg PA
CBHW070002180726
48002CB00019B/1882